kitchen know-how

by **Sainsbury's**

everything you need to create simple,
tasty meals from scratch

10 9 8 7 6 5 4 3 2 1

Published in 2012 by Ebury Press, an imprint of Ebury Publishing
A Random House Group Company

The Random House Group Limited Reg. No. 954009

Addresses for companies within the Random House Group can be found at
www.randomhouse.co.uk

A CIP catalogue record for this book is available from the British Library

The Random House Group Limited supports The Forest Stewardship Council®(FSC®),
the leading international forest certification organisation. Our books carrying the
FSC label are printed on FSC® certified paper. FSC is the only forest
certification scheme endorsed by the leading environmental organisations,
including Greenpeace. Our paper procurement policy can be found at
www.randomhouse.co.uk/environment

To buy other books at Sainsbury's, go to www.sainsburysentertainment.co.uk

Design and art direction: Smith & Gilmour
Food photography: Dan Jones
Food stylist: Emma Marsden
Prop stylist: Tamzin Ferdinando

For Sainsbury's
Books team: Sharon Nightingale; Phil Carroll
Nutrition: Annie Denny
Product development/Food safety: Susi Richards, Ben Lewis
Supply chain: Lee Scott.

Printed and bound in China by C & C Offset Printing Co., Ltd

ISBN 9780091949488

RECIPE NOTES

❄ Indicates a recipe is suitable for freezing

Butter is unsalted unless otherwise specified

Eggs are medium unless otherwise specified

Vegetables such as onions and garlic are always peeled unless specified

contents

The Essential Storecupboard

It's easy to fill your cupboards with lots of ingredients that you fancy, on a whim, while shopping. But the best way of making sure you have enough in to make dinner in the evening is to have a permanent stock of a good range of basics. That's a combination of items you know will always be in your cupboard, fridge and freezer and that can be mixed and matched to make delicious no-effort suppers. As long as you have the basics, you'll always have something to throw together to make a meal, and these basics can then be topped up with other ingredients you need to make your meals varied and interesting.

Eggs, cheese, milk and butter are your **fridge** essentials. With just a few other basics these can produce quick fixes for meals at any time of the day – from omelettes and scrambled eggs to cheese on toast or even a soufflé. Your fridge should also contain basic vegetables, such as onions, and protein basics such as ham, which can be used on its own in a sandwich or chopped and made into simple pasta dishes or salads (see pages 10–12 for quick stand-by supper suggestions).

By stocking your **storecupboard** with a good variety of long-life ingredients you'll have the all-important building blocks of a meal. Oil and vinegar are essential for cooking, while spices and dried herbs boost the flavour of a recipe. In addition, it's important to have a choice of pasta, rice and pulses, the filling foundations, around which you can build a dish.

Your **freezer** needs to have enough space to store freeze-ahead suppers, such as soups and stews. It should also contain basics that can be cooked straight from frozen, such as peas and bread (which can be toasted from frozen).

Below is a list of basic ingredients for your 'storecupboard'. They've been divided into 'essentials', 'handy to have in' and 'luxuries'. 'Essentials' are the fundamentals – ingredients without which you can't really cook. 'Handy to have in' are those that allow you to vary and expand your recipe repertoire, ensuring that you don't have to nip to the shops to make a meal complete. The 'luxury' items are the one-offs that enrich recipes and transform an everyday supper into something more special. Clearly every household is different, and while some people might consider jam to be a complete essential in their storecupboard, others may see it as something they only use from time to time. The ingredients have therefore been divided according to how fundamental they are to creating a meal.

The Fridge

Keep your fridge below 5°C. Ideally you should store ingredients on the appropriate shelves: any raw meat products should be placed on the bottom shelf, either in packaging or in sealable containers so blood doesn't drip onto any other items and contaminate them. Keep vegetables and salad in the drawers at the bottom of the fridge, which are specially designed to keep them crisp and fresher for longer. Cooked leftovers should be stored in sealable containers and eaten within two days.

FRIDGE ESSENTIALS

Eggs
Milk
Cheese (a hard cheese, such as Cheddar, for instant snacks, and Parmesan for grating over pasta, into risotto and flavouring vegetable-based soups)
Butter (salted is a good all-rounder as it keeps longer, but if you bake regularly make sure it's unsalted, and taste savoury dishes for seasoning)
Mayonnaise
Yoghurt (natural and fruit)
Ham

HANDY TO HAVE IN

Bacon
Sausages
Chicken pieces
Vegetarian alternative: tofu
Smoked mackerel fillets
Soft cream cheese
Greek-style yoghurt
Ginger
Green and red chillies
Carrots
Celery
Lettuce
Tomato
Cucumber
Broccoli
Lemon
Ready-made pastry (either filo or shortcrust for topping pies or making very quick tarts)

LUXURIES

Double cream
Crème fraîche
Smoked salmon trimmings
Parma ham

The Storecupboard

It's a good idea to have a list of what's in your storecupboard and stick it inside the cupboard door, so you can easily see what you have in. Cross off items when you've used them up or replace as necessary, which will prevent you wasting anything.

STORECUPBOARD ESSENTIALS

Oils (olive, sunflower or rapeseed oil for cooking; extra virgin olive oil dressings)

Salt

Black peppercorns

Rice – keep three different varieties of rice: Thai or basmati for Asian dishes; long-grain for serving with stews instead of potatoes; and risotto rice

Pasta – keep a long pasta, such as spaghetti, linguine or tagliatelle for smooth sauces such as a tomato or Bolognese sauce (see Spaghetti alla Carbonara, page 150; Spaghetti Bolognese, page 148; and Pasta Primavera, page 134); and a short pasta, such as farfalle (bows), penne (quills) or fusilli (twists), which are good for chunky sauces and can also be thrown into vegetable-rich soups and casseroles (see Penne with Olives, Anchovy and Chilli, page 140; and Pasta with Chorizo, page 152).

Noodles – both egg and rice noodles cook in minutes and are easy to prepare either by boiling or soaking them

Pulses – canned or dried chickpeas and kidney beans, Puy or green and red lentils and baked beans. (If using dried beans, remember you need to soak them in cold water overnight before simmering in boiling water until tender.)

Canned fish – a selection of tuna, salmon, anchovies, sardines, mackerel according to preference

Canned tomatoes – chopped or whole plum)

Tomato purée

Clear honey – for making sauces for stir-fries and marinating meat (see Garlic and Honey Pork with Vegetable Noodle Broth, page 106)

Mustard powder – it can be used powdered for cooking (see Pork Casserole with Mustard Dumplings, page 115; and Mushroom and Ale Casserole with Thyme Dumplings, page 168) or mixed with water for a wet mustard and served alongside a stew, such as Beef and Beer Stew with Buttery Mash, page 126.

Savoury condiments – Worcestershire sauce, tomato ketchup, soy sauce, redcurrant jelly

Vinegar – balsamic, white wine, cider or red wine, for dressings

Spices and seasoning – curry powder or paste, cumin, coriander, chilli flakes, chilli powder, dried bay leaves

Stock cubes or liquid stock – a selection of chicken (light chicken stock can also be used for fish dishes), vegetable and beef. Stock cubes need to be reconstituted with water and tend to be more highly seasoned, so take care when adding salt and pepper to your dish and adjust to your own taste.

Concentrated liquid stock needs to be diluted with water and similarly tasted for seasoning. Fresh stock can be found in the chilled aisles. It has a short shelf life but is ready to use.

Sugar – caster and light muscovado sugar

Baking ingredients – plain flour and baking powder

Bread – white or brown sliced

Potatoes

Onions

Garlic

HANDY TO HAVE IN

Other types of oil – sesame oil for dressing stir-fries; nut oils, such as walnut, for salad dressings

Spices – Chinese five spice, ground cinnamon, cinnamon sticks

Savoury condiments and preserves – horseradish sauce, mint sauce or jelly, fruit chutney, capers, gherkins, peanut butter, yeast extract

Savoury sauces and pastes – hoisin sauce, black bean sauce, sweet chilli dipping sauce, Thai green curry paste, harissa

Mustard – Dijon and wholegrain

Sweet preserves – jam, marmalade

Coconut milk – a creamy addition to Thai and Indian curries and can also give a softer flavour to spicy soups

Savoury biscuits – digestives, crackers, rice cakes

Other types of bread – flatbreads, tortillas and naan bread make great accompaniments to flesh out meals; they often come in a sealed pack with a long shelf life but once opened need to be eaten within two or three days or wrapped in plastic film and frozen for up to a month)

Poppadoms – buy uncooked; they can be cooked in minutes in the microwave (sprinkle with water and cook according to packet instructions)

Couscous – ready in minutes by rehydrating in a bowl using hot stock (see Tandoori Chicken with Minted Couscous, page 94), and any leftovers can be stored in the fridge for up to four days)

Lasagne sheets

Fresh herbs – growing pots of parsley, thyme or rosemary

Baking ingredients – vanilla extract, icing sugar, bread flour, dried active yeast

Cereal – porridge oats and muesli are useful for baking or quick puddings

Dried fruit– sultanas, dates, prunes (for cakes and biscuits and for chopping up and mixing with yogurt for breakfast or a snack)

Nuts and seeds – sesame seeds (great for stir-fries), almonds (chopped with fruit and yogurt), hazelnuts, brazil nuts, cashew nuts

Canned fruit – pineapple chunks, cherries, peaches.

Antipasto jars – marinated peppers, olives, sundried tomatoes, chargrilled artichokes – for layering up in sandwiches, scattering over pizzas or using in pasta sauces (see Pasta in a Rich Provençal Sauce, page 130; once a jar is opened, store in the fridge up to two weeks)

Miso paste – for quick clear vegetable soup and noodle-based Asian dishes

Quick-cook polenta – the variety that cooks in one minute makes an instant accompaniment

Dried mushrooms

Baking ingredients – ground almonds, chocolate (dark, white, milk), silver balls, demerara and dark muscovado sugar, food colouring (for decorating cakes)

Golden syrup

Treacle

Creamed coconut or coconut cream

Ground white pepper

The Freezer

Fill up your freezer drawers with these ingredients, but leave a drawer free so you can freeze cooked food, such as soups and stews, too.

FREEZER ESSENTIALS

Bread – sliced white or brown loaf, pitta bread

Frozen peas

Sausages – wrapped in portions of two or four, and vegetarian options

Bacon – wrapped in portions of four rashers

Skinless chicken breasts or turkey escalopes – wrapped in two-portion parcels

Portions of fish and /or seafood mixes

Beef /vegetarian mince

HANDY TO HAVE IN

Frozen prawns

Chopped vegetables and frozen spinach

Breadcrumbs

LUXURIES

Frozen fruit

Good-quality vanilla ice cream

Oven chips or potato wedges

10 Quick-Fix Recipes

By stocking your storecupboard as described on pages 5–9, you'll always have a meal in hand. Here are 10 easy recipes to get you started. Quantities simply need to be adapted according to the number of people you're feeding.

SIMPLE HAM AND PEA PASTA

This is just as easy as it sounds. Start by slicing an onion and sauté in olive oil and a small knob of butter until softened. Chop a couple of slices of ham and stir in. Throw in a handful of frozen peas or any finely chopped vegetables you have to hand with a sprig of rosemary or thyme. Drizzle over some water and a splash of balsamic vinegar, cover and leave to simmer gently while you cook a pan of pasta until al dente (tender but firm to the bite), or according to packet instructions. Drain the pasta well, return to the pan and add the ham sauce. Drizzle over extra virgin olive oil and toss well, then season with a little grated Parmesan and some freshly ground black pepper.

STUFFED JACKETS

Cut baking potatoes in half lengthways. Brush all over with oil and bake in a preheated oven at 200°C/180°Fan/Mark 6 for about 40–50 minutes until the potato in the middle is tender. Take out of the oven and use a spoon to scoop out most of the filling into a bowl, leaving a shell of potato still in the skins. Mash the filling with butter, a spoonful of wholegrain mustard, grated cheese and any herbs you have to hand. If you have a tomato that needs using up, chop that up, too, and mix it in. Return the filling to the skins, sprinkle with a little extra grated cheese and grill under a medium grill until bubbling.

EGG FRIED RICE

This is ready in minutes if you have leftover rice (if you don't, cook the rice according to packet instructions). Drizzle a little oil into a wok and add the cooked rice. Push the rice to one side of the pan, then add beaten eggs to the other side. Tip the pan over the heat to cook the eggs, stirring them as you do to scramble them. Gradually add the rice into the mixture and add some thawed frozen peas. Toss everything together, then drizzle with soy sauce and sweet chilli sauce, if you have it.

SPECIAL OMELETTE

Turn a simple omelette into a treat. Beat a couple of eggs and season well. Melt a knob of butter in a large frying pan and throw in a handful of spinach. Cook until just wilted. Remove and set aside. Add the eggs to the pan and tilt it around so the mixture covers the base. Set the pan over the heat and use a wooden spoon to draw the egg across the base, then tilt the pan to allow the runny mixture to run into the holes. Continue to do this until all of the mixture is set. Spoon the spinach into the middle with some chopped ham and grated cheese, flip over one side, then slide onto a plate.

MOROCCAN VEGGIE STEW

This is a great way to make use of wilted veg in the bottom of the fridge. Chop a mixture of vegetables (onions, carrots, celery, pepper, squash, leeks and aubergine and broccoli stalks are ideal) into even-sized pieces. Put in a large pan with a drizzle of oil. Cook over a medium heat for 10 minutes until the vegetables have softened and are starting to caramelise. Stir in a heaped teaspoon of harissa. (If you don't have any harissa, stir in ½ teaspoon each of cumin, coriander and paprika with a pinch of chilli flakes and a good squirt of tomato purée.) Add a can of drained chickpeas and enough chicken or vegetable stock to cover. Put a lid on the pan and simmer for 20 minutes. Serve with couscous.

ITALIAN RICE AND PEAS

This is a simple version of Italy's basic but delicious soupy rice dish, *risi e bisi*. Cook a finely chopped onion in olive oil until soft. Stir in a crushed garlic clove and cook for a minute or so. Stir in risotto rice and cook for a few minutes until translucent. Over a gentle heat, add hot chicken or vegetable stock, according to the quantities on the packet, one ladle at a time. Allow each to be absorbed into the rice before adding the next. The rice is ready when all the stock has been used up and it feels soft but still has a slight bite. The mixture should still look soupy. Stir in thawed, frozen peas, grated Parmesan and chopped parsley and season well with salt and pepper.

BANGER IN A 'BUN'

Make your sausages go further by combining them with other ingredients from your storecupboard. Slice an onion and sauté in olive oil until very soft – about 20 minutes. Stir in a splash of balsamic vinegar and a pinch of light muscovado sugar. Slice sausages in half lengthways and fry, cut-side down first, in a pan until thoroughly cooked. Slice a tomato, shred some lettuce, then stuff into a split, toasted pitta with a little of the sautéed onion. Fill with the sausage and enjoy.

STIR-FRIED CHICKEN

A quick-cook dish that can be varied according to what you have in your fridge. Slice chicken breast or thigh into finger-width pieces and marinate in grated ginger, crushed garlic, honey and soy sauce. For a bit of spice, add a chopped red chilli to the mixture or a good pinch of chilli flakes. Leave to marinate for at least 30 minutes. Heat a little oil in a pan or wok and stir-fry the chicken over a medium heat until golden. Add broccoli, cut into florets, and carrots, chopped into matchsticks. Drizzle over a little water, cover the pan and allow the vegetables to steam and finish cooking. Serve with rice or noodles.

ANTIPASTI COUSCOUS

Pour some couscous into a bowl and add the same volume of hot vegetable or chicken stock. Cover and set aside to soak. Finely chop any antipasti – peppers, artichokes or olives – and put in a bowl with leftover shredded roast chicken. Drizzle over extra virgin olive oil and squeeze in the juice of half a lemon. Fluff up the couscous, stir in the chicken mixture and some chopped herbs. Season with salt and pepper, then serve.

PRAWN SPAGHETTI

Cook spaghetti in a pan of boiling water cook until al dente, or according to packet instructions. Drain the pasta and return to the pan with a little water clinging to the pasta. Stir in lemon zest and a good squeeze of lemon juice, a pinch of chilli flakes, some crème fraîche, chopped wilted spinach and thawed frozen prawns.

Your Essential Kitchen Kit

A good selection of equipment and utensils is essential for all regular cooks. Whether you're rustling up a quick midweek supper or making a more challenging recipe, they're the tools that will help you get the job done.

Below is a list of general kitchen equipment (the nuts and bolts of the kit), a range of pans and baking specifics you may need and, finally, some electrical gadgets, which will make the preparation of recipes easier. Not everything here is essential, but it all has a value, and the more experienced a cook you become, the more you will discover how to make each individual item work best for you. Before buying any equipment, consider how much you are going to use it. If it's going to be used a lot, with lots of wear and tear, buy the best you can afford so it will last. If it's a one-off gadget, you can plump for one that is cheaper.

Kitchen Utensils and General Equipment

This list may look long, but it includes all the essentials needed for everyday cooking. Store cooking spoons in pots on display in your kitchen, or in drawers, but make sure you store the knives separately, in a safe place.

Knives: you'll need a small knife for peeling and chopping small fruit and vegetables, such as shallots; a medium knife for chopping and slicing larger quantities of ingredients (a pile of herbs, a bar of chocolate, a handful of nuts, etc.) and preparing vegetables, such as onions, carrots and celery; a large carving knife and a serrated knife for cutting bread

Chopping boards: keep three – one for fruit and vegetables; one for bread, baked and cooked ingredients; and one for raw meat and fish

Wooden spoons: keep three – two for stirring savoury dishes and one for baking

Large metal spoon: for folding ingredients together for a cake and for serving mashed potato and stews straight from the pot

Weighing scales: electric are the most accurate and the easiest to use, particularly when baking

Measuring spoons

Measuring jug

Spatulas: two sizes – small, for scraping ingredients out of jars; and medium, for scraping pans and bowls of cake mixture so nothing is wasted

Colander

Tin opener

Peeler

Garlic crusher

Potato masher

Whisk

Ladle

Turkey baster

Grater

Fish slice: useful for lifting and serving fillets and whole fish

Palette knife: for transferring biscuits from baking sheets to a cooling rack

Ruler: for measuring the base of cake tins and cutting out greaseproof and baking parchment

Metal or wooden skewers

Plastic film

Tin foil

Oven gloves

Tea towels

Plastic, sealable containers for chilling and freezing food.

Pans and Roasting Tins

As a minimum you'll need a small, medium and large pan, each with a lid. Heavy-based pans have a thicker bottom so are better for conducting the heat and are more likely to ensure the food doesn't cook too quickly. When frying or softening onions or vegetables in oil or butter, place the pan over a medium–low heat (rather than a high heat) so it comes up to temperature gradually. This ensures the ingredients are less likely to burn when they're put into the pan. When you're buying pans, make sure they sit steady when empty and are the right size for the rings on your hob.

Medium frying pan (base of around 20cm)
Wok
Griddle pan
Ovenproof casserole pan with lid
Small and medium roasting tin
Meat roasting tin with rack
Steamer: handy for cooking fish in a flash and a healthy method for preparing vegetables. A steamer that sits on top of a pan base (which can be filled with water to steam) and is used on the hob is the most useful. Consider buying an electric steamer if you cook a lot of food using this method, and also if you have the space to store it. A two-tier wooden oriental steamer with a lid is best used in a wok and is handy if you're tight for space.

Baking Equipment

Whether you're baking biscuits, a loaf of bread or a batch of scones, the list below includes a range of equipment that will be useful for making a variety of different recipes. If you're a novice baker, not everything here will be essential, so try to consider how much you're going to use these items and establish your budget accordingly.

Bowls: small, medium and large. Glass or metal is preferable to plastic, which marks easily and harbours grease.
Two large baking sheets: one flat, one lipped – the latter is handy for biscuits so they don't slide off
Cake tins: 900g loaf tin, 20cm deep springform cake tin, sandwich cake tins – either 18cm or 20cm
12-hole deep muffin tin
12-hole bun tin
Ramekins
Loose-bottomed fluted metal quiche tin for baking sweet and savoury tarts
Scone cutters: buy the double-sided set so there's a choice of the round cutter for shaping scones and crinkled edge for biscuits
Rolling pin
Cake slice
Palette knife
Piping bag and a selection of round and star nozzles for piping biscuits and piping icing
Baking beans for blind baking
Cooling rack
Sieve: for sifting flour to make it lighter and for dusting icing sugar over bakes.

Baking parchment
Greaseproof paper
Oven thermometer – to check the temperature accurately.

Baking parchment and greaseproof paper – what's the difference?

Baking parchment is coated with silicone on both sides, which gives it a non-stick surface and means that anything placed on it will slip off. It is used for lining trays when baking biscuits and meringues as you can slide them off easily, or, in the case of meringues, peel them off. It is also useful for steaming (see recipe for Asian-style Fish Parcels, page 77) and for wrapping foods for freezing. Greaseproof paper has a natural barrier to grease and oily foods. When baking a cake, greaseproof paper should be used to line the tin as it ensures the cake will have the same texture on the outside as the inside (parchment repels the cake and thus hardens the outside). It is particularly useful for wrapping baked fruit cakes, which need to be stored for several months, to keep them moist, and fed with alcohol to enrich them.

Electrical gadgets

As well as considering how much you are likely to use these items before investing in them, it's also important to ensure you have enough storage for them and, in the case of the food processor, that it's easy to lift in and out of a cupboard if it's not going to sit on a kitchen counter.

Hand blender: useful if you make and freeze big batches of soup. Pick one with a metal stem so it can be put into hot liquid straight away without waiting for the liquid to cool down.

Electric hand whisk: for creaming butter and sugar together quickly when baking and for whipping cream.

Microwave: for melting butter and chocolate easily, defrosting and reheating frozen food quickly.

Food processor: this electrical appliance consists of a jug and lid that fit on top of an electrical motor and comes complete with several blades. It is an expensive purchase but is valuable for simplifying several cooking tasks. There is a blade, which blends chunky soups (cool these a little first and blend in batches otherwise the mixture can explode from the jug); the main two-wing blade makes light work of the first stage of shortcrust pastry, cutting the butter into the flour (traditionally this was done by the labour-intensive method of chopping the butter through the flour using two knives); several disc blades chop vegetables for coleslaw and help you to prepare large batches of chopped or sliced onions, and food processors also come with a plastic dough hook (for bread).

Cooking Techniques

Although some of this section may not seem relevant to more accomplished cooks, learning a range of cooking techniques and understanding the principles behind them and how they affect your cooking is key to getting the best out of a recipe. Even the most confident cooks might benefit from a glance through the definitions below, which take you through some basic foundations of cookery, from baking and braising to steaming and stir-frying.

Baking

This method of cooking uses the oven to cook savoury and sweet dishes, such as biscuits, bread, cakes, pies, tarts and quiches.

The temperature of the oven can be varied during cooking, for example with pastry quiches and tarts it is heated to a high temperature at the start of the cooking time in order to harden and bake the 'crust' (the pastry) and later reduced to cook the filling slowly without it curdling or burning the outer edge (see Creamy Leek Tart, page 184). The methods of baking and roasting (see definition on page 26) are very similar in that dishes are both cooked in the oven. Where they differ, however, is that baking tends to refer to dishes that need to be cooked to become edible, for example raw bread or biscuit dough, and pastry. Baking is also used to refer to recipes that need to rise or puff up. In contrast, roasting tends to refer to whole ingredients, such as meat, fish and vegetables, which are covered first with a little oil to help to flavour and caramelise the finished dish. (An exception to this definition, however, is baked potatoes, sometimes known as jacket potatoes, as these don't require any fat to cook them, although brushing them with oil does help crisp up the skin).

Before baking any dish, the oven should be preheated to the correct temperature. Cakes should be placed into a medium oven: the initial burst of heat helps the mixture to rise and later the sugar to caramelise. At the same time as this is happening, the heat is drying out the inside, ensuring it cooks evenly all the way through. Although the outside of a cake is firmer than the soft, sponge of the interior, it shouldn't be crisp (see Chocolate Fudge Cake, page 223).

Biscuits are cooked at a medium temperature too, and in this case the dry heat from the oven crisps up the base and draws out the moisture from the dough (see Double Chocolate Cookies, page 218; and Spiced Finger Biscuits, page 217).

The temperature for baking bread varies depending on the recipe. For example, pizza dough requires a high temperature for it to be cooked quickly so that the base becomes hard-baked and crisp. For crusty loaves, a high temperature is called for at the beginning, to give the dough a burst of heat for an initial rise and to firm up the crust, then it is reduced to a medium temperature for the remaining baking time. In other recipes, where the finished bread has a soft crust, the bread is baked at a medium temperature all the way through the cooking time (see A Simple Loaf, page 231; and Fruit Bread, page 232). Professional bakers use steam ovens to keep bread moist, and this effect can be replicated at home by putting a roasting tin of boiling water underneath the loaf before baking or spraying the sides of the oven with water.

Braising

This is a method of slow-cooking tough cuts of meat to tenderise them. There are two stages – first the meat is seared over a high heat, which browns it and seals the flavour, then it is placed in a lidded pot with liquid, generally stock or wine, either on the hob, over a very low heat, or in the oven, at a low temperature. The meat cooks very slowly for several hours, which results in a tender texture (see Pork Casserole with Mustard Dumplings, page 115; Beef and Beer Stew with Buttery Mash, page 126; Lamb Shanks with Redcurrant and Rosemary, page 120). This method is similar to pot-roasting, where a whole joint is placed in the pot, but very little or no liquid is used and the resulting dish has a roasted appearance and taste.

To give added flavour to the joint and the resulting juices, the meat may be placed over a thin layer of finely chopped vegetables, usually onions, carrot and celery, that have been sautéed in the same pan in oil and butter until they are evenly golden.

Cuts suitable for braising are beef chuck, shin, brisket, neck and silverside; lamb shoulder, neck, scrag and breast; pork leg and venison shoulder (see pages 35–9 for more information about the different cuts of meat).

Braising vegetables is a similar method, but has a slightly different execution, and is most suitable for winter vegetables, such as carrots, onions, cabbage (red and green, such as Savoy) and celery. The vegetable is fried first in a little butter, to flavour it, then cooked in a smaller quantity of stock than meat, which steams and makes it tender.

Frying

Frying means to cook food in hot fat or oil, either in a low-sided frying pan (shallow-frying) or in a large quantity of oil in a saucepan or deep-fat fryer (deep-frying).

To shallow-fry, pour a thin layer of oil (or other fat, such as butter or lard) into a frying pan and make sure it's heated before placing any food in the pan. The oil is hot enough when ingredients sizzle as they come into contact with it. The heat underneath the pan should be medium–high; it's important that the oil isn't smoking hot, however, or it will burn the food rather than brown it (although see Searing, below, for the exception to this). Fry food in batches, so the temperature of the pan maintains an even heat throughout. If too many pieces are placed in the pan at the same time, the temperature will drop and the food will steam rather than fry in the oil. Once the ingredient has cooked on the outside, turn down the heat to allow the inside to cook.

When shallow-frying delicate pieces of fish it is a good idea to coat the fillet in flour first (or fry it *à la meunière*, to use the French term) to prevent it falling apart (see Seared Cod with Wilted Spinach on page 79). This also crisps up the outside. It is not always essential, though, when cooking whole fish or a fillet of fat-rich fish, such as salmon or mackerel. Flouring meat before cooking may be required in some recipes, but isn't essential.

To deep fry, use an oil with a high smoking point, such as corn oil. (The smoking point is the point at which the oil gets so hot that it starts to break down and smoke.) Pour the oil into a large, deep pan, making sure there is space at the top for the oil to bubble up once heated. While the oil is heating, don't cover the pan with a lid and never leave pans unattended. You will need to heat the oil to a temperature that should be specified in the recipe (temperatures vary depending on whether meat, fish or vegetables are being cooked). Food should be dry and at room temperature to prevent splattering. Gradually lower three or four small pieces of food or one large ingredient into the hot oil. As with shallow frying, too many pieces in the pan will cause the temperature of the oil to drop and the food will taste greasy rather than crisp on the outside and moist on the inside.

Sautéeing is a method of lightly frying ingredients, for example onions or shallots, celery, carrots and garlic, for a soup, stew or sauce. They are browned first in oil and sometimes butter, then cooked with stock and other vegetables, plus meat or fish.

Searing is where the outside of the ingredient – usually meat or fish – is cooked first in a pan at a high temperature to caramelise it. It is also sometimes called 'browning' (see Seared Tuna with a Sweet and Sour Marinade, page 80).

Grilling

There are two ways to grill: one is used to cook meat, fish, vegetables and bread (as toast) under a layer of heat; the other is to sear these ingredients quickly on a preheated griddle pan (a pan that looks like a frying pan but has a ridged base).

When grilling food under the grill, it is important to watch it carefully. One minute too long and the food can turn from being perfectly golden and edible to being burnt and unpalatable. In contrast, when cooking on a griddle, it is best to stand back and allow the ingredients to cook and be sealed by the heat of the hot pan until a golden crust forms.

Small cuts of tender meat, such as chicken breast and thighs, beef steaks, lamb cutlets and pork chops, or fillets of fish are suitable for grilling, as are firm-textured vegetables, such as onions, aubergines, peppers and courgettes. The pieces are thinner so the high heat of the grill cooks them quickly. Cooking them on a griddle will create an even pattern of dark golden ridges where the meat or fish has caramelised – this is not only attractive, it tastes delicious, too.

Make sure the food is at room temperature before grilling so that it cooks evenly all the way through. If it's fridge-cold when it goes into the pan, it'll take longer to cook and the inside could dry out. Take it out of the fridge at least half an hour before cooking, and use tongs or a fish slice and fork to turn the ingredients over and cook all sides. (For grilled recipes, see Tandoori Chicken with Minted Couscous, page 94; Gammon Steaks with a Cucumber, Mango and Chilli Salsa, page 113).

Poaching

This method involves submerging an ingredient in liquid, whereby the heat is turned down to a low setting so that the liquid is only very gently moving. It is used for a range of different ingredients, from large to small, but the principle is the same. Poaching prevents the structure of the ingredient breaking up while cooking.

To poach an egg, for example, the water should be brought to a simmer so it is hot, but when the egg is dropped in it should be barely trembling. Once the egg is in the water, the heat immediately sets the outside and then continues to cook the white gently until it is set. This principle also applies to cooking delicate fish, whereby the poaching liquor used may either be water, milk or stock and can be flavoured with herbs such as bay, a few slices of onion and black peppercorns.

The texture of meat, whether it is a small or large piece, is dense. Poaching is used in these instances to tenderise and give a more succulent texture to the finished dish (see Pea and Ham Soup, page 49).

For fruit, namely pears and stoned fruit, such as peaches and apricots, the method is used so that the fruit cooks gently all the way through and remains whole after cooking. The poaching liquor may be either a sugar syrup, fruit juice or alcohol.

Poaching is sometimes required as part of another recipe, such as dumplings (see Pork Casserole with Mustard Dumplings, page 115; and Mushroom and Ale Casserole with Thyme Dumplings, page 168), where the cooking liquid for the primary part of the dish simmers very gently to cook them, rather than bubbling fiercely which may break them up.

Roasting

Similar to baking, roasting uses an oven to cook meat, fish or vegetables, and sometimes fruit, over a long cooking time. A drizzle of oil – and sometimes other seasonings, such as mustard, spices and dried herbs – is rubbed over the ingredient so that the outside caramelises while the inside remains juicy and tender (see recipe for Roast Chicken, page 99; and Garlic and Honey Pork with Vegetable Noodle Broth, page 106). If roasting fruit, use a knob of butter rather than oil, and add a sprinkling of sugar to help caramelise.

It's important to rest meat after roasting to allow time for the juices to run through it. This leaves the joint more tender and easier to carve as a result.

To rest meat, put it on a warm plate, cover loosely with foil and set aside for 5–10 minutes for small cuts or 15–30 minutes for larger joints.

Steaming

This is a very healthy method of cooking because the food is cooked very gently and lightly, which means it loses fewer vitamins and minerals. Water is heated in a pan to create steam and the ingredients are placed above it in a separate receptacle to cook them. The food doesn't touch the water and may be placed directly into a steamer resting over a pan or wrapped and sealed in a parcel first. It is ideal for cooking tender pieces of fish or shellfish and for vegetables, which don't have a dense texture so cook quickly in the heat (see Asian-style Fish Parcels, page 77).

There are several devices you can use for steaming. A metal steamer consists of two or more parts. A solid-based pan sits on the hob and above or inside it sits a receptacle – or several tiers of receptacles – that has holes in it (the steamer part). The whole device is then covered with

Stir-frying

a lid. A bamboo steamer is similar but comes complete with its own lid and can be different sizes – either large or small – and can also be built up with many layers. It sits in a wok or pan, in which water is heated to create the steam. An electrical steamer is a one-piece gadget that sits on the kitchen work surface and is plugged in. Again it consists of several layers (usually three) so that you can cook different ingredients on each level.

Steaming can also be used to describe the cooking technique whereby an ingredient is placed in a lidded pot with just a small amount of liquid in the bottom. The liquid is still heated to boiling, to create steam. The steam circulates within the pot and cooks the dish (see Steamed Mussels with White Wine Sauce, page 90).

In traditional stir-fries, meat, fish or vegetables are cooked in a wok very quickly over a high heat with only a little oil, so the meat or fish is tender and cooked through but the vegetables retain a slight bite. The small base and deep sides mean a wok has a larger surface area than a conventional frying pan, so it heats up quickly and maintains the heat. The ingredients are constantly tossed around the base and sides of the pan to cook them rapidly.

Ingredients should be cut to the same size so they cook evenly, and meat needs to be added to the pan first as it has the longest cooking time. When cooking the vegetables, add the firm-textured vegetables, such as carrots and peppers, first, as these require longer cooking, then add the softer ones (such as pak choi or spinach) towards the end of the cooking time. (For recipes using the stir-frying technique see Stir-fried King Prawns on Sesame Noodles, page 82; and Chinese-style Vegetable Noodles, page 164).

27

Buying & Storing Fresh Produce

Fresh food, bought at its peak, will always have the most flavour and will ensure, whichever way it is cooked, that the end result tastes the best. Here's what to look for when choosing and buying a range of fresh ingredients.

Vegetables

When choosing produce, look for fruit and vegetables free from any blemishes and that feel heavy for their size when you pick them up. This is when they're still full of goodness and water, before they start to decay. The skin should look smooth and fresh – almost as if it's just been picked. If it's wrinkled, shows any early signs of rotting (in the form of brown spots on aubergines, for example) or the leaves look limp (cauliflowers or broccoli), it is past its best. When you're buying any kind of potato, check for smooth skins and discard any that have growths or eyes sprouting on them or have a green tinge to their skins. It is best to buy vegetables that are in season, when they are most plentiful, as this is the time they will have the most flavour.

Store green vegetables, including lettuce, green beans, cauliflower and the like, in the vegetable drawers, which are the warmest part of the fridge.

Tomatoes should be kept at room temperature as refrigeration dulls their flavour and ripeness. Instead, place them in a sunny spot near a window or in a warm place in the kitchen with plenty of air around them so they continue to ripen naturally.

Onions, shallots, garlic and ginger can all be kept in a bowl in the kitchen, too, or in a cool dry place.

Store potatoes in a cool, dark place. If possible, put them inside a canvas potato bag, which allows the air to circulate around them, and use within a week.

Packets of herbs, except basil, should be kept in the fridge. If buying herbs in pots, place them out of direct sunlight and water daily.

29

Fruit

The principles for choosing vegetables apply to fruit, too. Pick up whole fruit and feel the weight in your hand to check it feels heavy for its size. Store in a bowl in the kitchen, away from the light, which may cause fruit to ripen too quickly and then go off. You can keep fruits in the fridge, too, but refrigeration can dull their flavour so remember to take them out of the fridge about an hour before you want to eat them to allow them to come to room temperature and enhance the taste.

Summer fruits, such as strawberries, raspberries and blueberries, should look fresh, not mushy, be free from any watery spots, and smell of their essence. Store them in the fridge and enjoy within two days. Wash just before use and keep strawberries with their stalks intact so they'll last longer.

Exotic fruits need a little extra attention when you're choosing them. Passion fruit should be wrinkled – this is when the juice will be at its sweetest. When the outside is smooth and shiny, the inside will taste quite tart.

The colour of mangoes does not determine their ripeness. Mangoes vary from green, yellow and red and any combination of all three. To check whether a mango is ready to eat, squeeze it gently and it should yield slightly under pressure. Have a good sniff around the stalk, too. It should smell fruity – just like a mango! To ripen at home, put one in a brown paper bag with an apple, then store in the fridge

as soon as it has ripened to prevent it from ripening any further.

Honeydew melons have a pale creamy yellow skin (rather than pale green) when they're ready to eat, and the bottom (the opposite end to the stalk end) will feel slightly soft when pushed. Canteloupe melons may have a subtle fruity/floral aroma and the outer skin should be a pale green, turning to yellow. Both these varieties can be shaken to test for ripeness, too. If they're ready, you can hear the seeds rattling inside.

A ripe watermelon is free from any blemishes or soft parts and will have a yellow or white bottom. You can also check its ripeness by slapping it with the palm of your hand: it should sound hollow.

Ripe pineapples have healthy, green leaves and are bright golden around the base, graduating up the body of the fruit to be combination of gold and green tinges. Once all the green parts have gone and the pineapple has turned bronze, it is overripe. Check the skin feels firm and is not wrinkled and mushy, and smell the base for a fruity, pineapple aroma.

Bananas ripen quickly when stored beside other fruit, so keep them in a separate bowl at room temperature (resist putting them in the fridge or they'll turn black). Once black spots start to appear on the skin, they're on the turn but this is the best time to use them in recipes (see Date and Banana Loaf, page 214). They'll have a full fruity banana flavour and be ultra sweet.

Fish and Shellfish

The smell of fish is the best indicator of its freshness – if it smells overly fishy, it is probably stale. Fresh fish should have a pleasant and delicate aroma of the sea. When buying whole fish, check that their eyes look bright, their gills are a fresh red colour and the flesh plump. If buying fillets, check that the flesh of the fish is unbroken and that it looks appetising.

Fish can also be smoked to preserve it. Cold smoking partially cooks the fish, so it still needs to be poached or grilled afterwards. Haddock and kippers are often cold smoked. There are two different types of smoked haddock – undyed and dyed. Undyed haddock is smoked over a wood fire in a kiln, which gives it its charismatic pale yellow colour. Dyed haddock is, just as the name suggests, made yellow with a smoke flavouring using modern processing methods. Hot smoking cooks the fish completely so it can be eaten as it is or, depending on the variety, made into a pâté. Mackerel, salmon, kippers, halibut, trout, tuna, prawns, cod roe and eel are often hot smoked.

Stocks for some fish are running low in certain parts of the world, and if overfished, may not be there in years to come for us to enjoy. To help maintain fish species, look for the MSC eco-label. This is a certification by the Marine Stewardship Council (www.msc.org) that ensures the fish you're eating is sustainable.

Shellfish such as raw mussels, lobsters, langoustine, crayfish and crab should be live before cooking. Lobsters will be a deep blue or grey, sometimes with pink tinges, and still be moving (their claws will be secured with elastic bands). They can be put to sleep by freezing prior to cooking, then either plunged into a pan of boiling water, live, or killed immediately before cooking by inserting a skewer or sharp knife into the head just behind the eyes. Once cooked, split in half and remove the stomach and intestines and enjoy the white meat and green liver.

Crabs vary in colour from blue–grey to pink and white. Send them to sleep first before killing by putting them in the freezer for two hours. They can then be cooked by being placed in a pan of cold salted water, covered with a lid, brought gently to the boil.

Raw mussels need to be cleaned before cooking and you will need to check they are still alive. Put them in a bowl of cold water, lightly scrub the shells and pull off any beards. These are the stringy strands attached to the mussels, which they use to cling on to the rocks as they grow. Tap each lightly to see if they close. If they do, they're safe to eat. If they remain open or have cracked shells, discard them.

Crayfish are much smaller than lobsters but similarly are blue–grey before cooking and turn pink afterwards. Again they should be cooked live. Langoustine are slightly bigger but stay the same colour once cooked as raw. Avoid ones that have a black tail as this indicates that they are already dead. Both can be simmered in boiling water to cook. Crayfish are good pan-fried on their own simply with butter or with a base of vegetables and wine; langoustine can be grilled.

Raw prawns should have a natural grey colour. Avoid those that look dry and have cracked or broken shells.

Scallops, whether presented in their shells or out of them and with or without the orange coral (the roe), should look plump and appetising. The roe is the eggs of the scallop and, if attached, should similarly look fresh. It has a smooth texture and creamy delicate flavour.

Prepared fillets of fresh fish should ideally be cooked and enjoyed either on the day they are bought or the next day. A whole fish, with its guts still intact, will be fine for up to two days, provided it is very fresh when bought.

Smoked fish can be stored in the fridge for up to two days. If the fish has been vacuum-packed, enjoy before the use-by date. Chill fish as soon as you get it home and place on the bottom shelf, on a plate if necessary, where any drips won't contaminate any other ingredients.

Squid can be bought either whole, just the body (which looks like a white sac) or already prepared and cut into rings. If buying whole, it needs to be prepared before cooking. Put it on a board and hold the body in one hand and tentacles in the other. Gently pull the tentacles out and with that will come the innards and quill (the central bone which looks and feels like plastic). Cut the tentacles away from the head by slicing just above the eyes and remove the beak from the tentacles (similarly this feels hard like the quill and is inedible; discard the eyes). Clean away the dark purplish skin from the main body and wash under cold water. Cut off the wings and set to one side as these are edible. Slice the body into rings, or cut down one edge to open the body out and score lightly in a criss-cross pattern, then pan-fry as a whole with the tentacles and reserved wings.

Fish can be classified into three categories: round fish, flat fish and shellfish.

ROUND FISH

So-called because the body is round, these fish have an eye on each side of their heads, the backbone runs the length of the body and there is a fillet on each side of it. Varieties include anchovy, cod, coley, gurnard, haddock, hake, herring, huss (also known as dogfish, rock and rock salmon), John Dory, ling, mackerel, monkfish, mullet (red and grey), pollack, salmon, sardine, sea bass, sea bream, snapper, sprat, swordfish, trout, tuna and whiting

FLAT FISH

The name comes from the shape of the fish: it is flat, with two eyes on the top of the head. When flat fish are spawned, the spawn that starts to grow look just like round fish. However as they develop, the body adapts and the guts twist, making one eye move round to join the other. At this stage, the fish move from the middle of the waters to the bottom of the lake or sea and the top of their skin becomes camouflaged to protect them from predators. Varieties include brill, halibut, plaice, ray, skate, sole (Dover and lemon) and turbot.

SHELLFISH

Shellfish have skeletons on the outside and they don't have a backbone. Varieties include clams, cockles, crabs, crayfish, cuttlefish, lobster, mussels, octopus, oysters, prawns, scallops, squid, whelks and winkles.

Poultry and Meat

Chicken, duck, goose, guinea fowl, poussin and turkey come under the banner of poultry.

You can buy chicken in a variety of forms. Chicken breasts and thighs (both are available to buy with or without skin and bones) cook quickly and you can buy them in the quantities you need. Wings and drumsticks provide less meat but are perfect left to marinate for at least a couple of hours, then roasted or grilled on a barbecue. They're the cheaper cuts from the bird so are ideal if you're on a budget and need to feed a crowd of people. Whole chicken is ideal for roasting in the oven or for pot-roasting (in a pan on the hob or in the oven and with vegetables and stock). Free-range and organic chickens (whatever the cut) tend to look thinner and less plump than battery-farmed birds and often have a slightly creamy appearance to the skin (unless corn-fed, where it will be tinged golden yellow). Poussins (baby chickens aged 4–6 weeks) will either have pink–white skin or, if they have been corn-fed, will be yellow.

Duck and goose differ from other poultry in that their flesh is dark. Duck has a dark red meat and creamy white dry skin. Goose has a thick covering of white skin and the meat underneath, if showing, tends to be slightly paler but still an obvious pink. The fat on each of these meats is rich. It is best to prick it well or score it before cooking to render it down (see Pan-Fried Duck with a Sour Cherry and Five-spice Sauce, page 104).

Guinea fowl, once wild and classed as game, is now farmed. It is smaller than a chicken and very lean. The skin should look dry and have a slight yellow tinge. The flesh, which sometimes shows through, is a slightly deeper pink than that of chicken.

Turkeys are at least three times the size of chickens, and the breasts and legs appear much more plump and rounded. Look for firm, dry, white skin.

Beef, lamb and pork are all classed as red meat but vary slightly in colour. Whether you're buying cuts from the meat counter (see pages 35–9 for more information about the different cuts) or in sealed packs, here's what to look for. Beef should be red and dull-looking, and if it has a covering of fat, this should look creamy. Pork should be pale pink (with no hint of grey) and, in contrast, the fat should be white. Lamb is a similar red to beef – although it differs depending on the age and breed of the animal; again the fat should look creamy.

Offal refers to the extras that come from butchering a whole animal. It is made up of the entrails and internal organs, including the liver, heart, kidneys, sweetbreads and tripe. The blanket term 'giblets' for poultry includes neck, gizzard, heart and liver. All should be eaten very fresh – look for pieces that are shiny and plump and avoid any that look dry.

Game is a term given to types of meat that have been hunted for sport

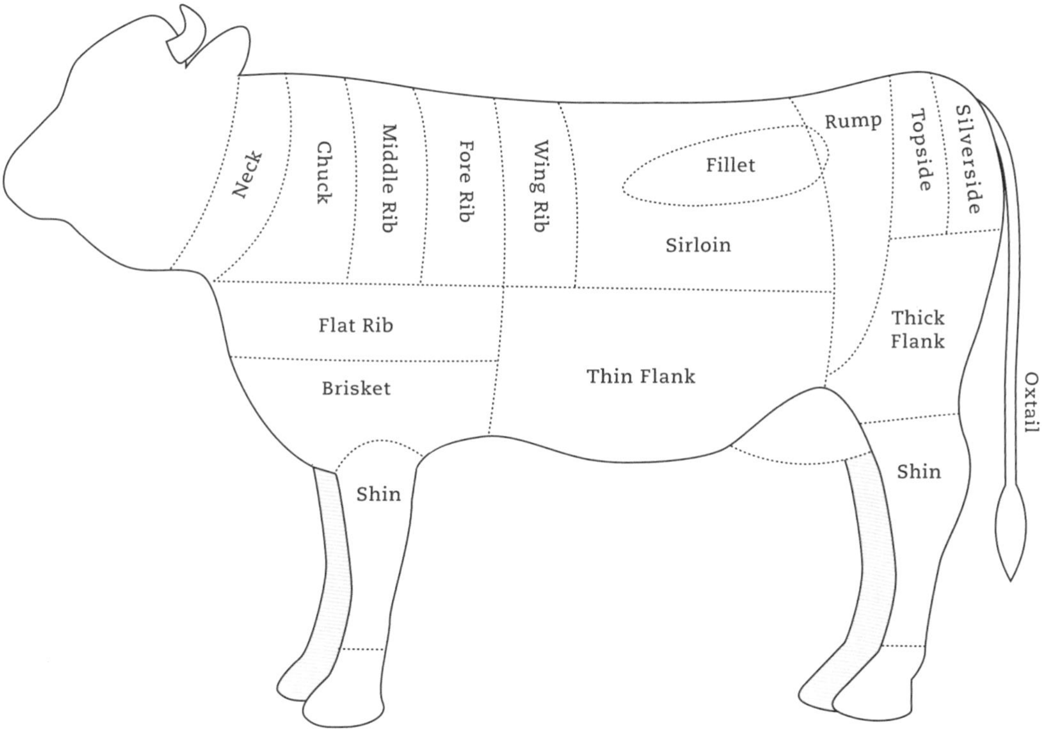

Beef

Neck · Chuck · Middle Rib · Fore Rib · Wing Rib · Rump · Topside · Silverside · Fillet · Sirloin · Flat Rib · Thick Flank · Brisket · Thin Flank · Oxtail · Shin · Shin

Pork

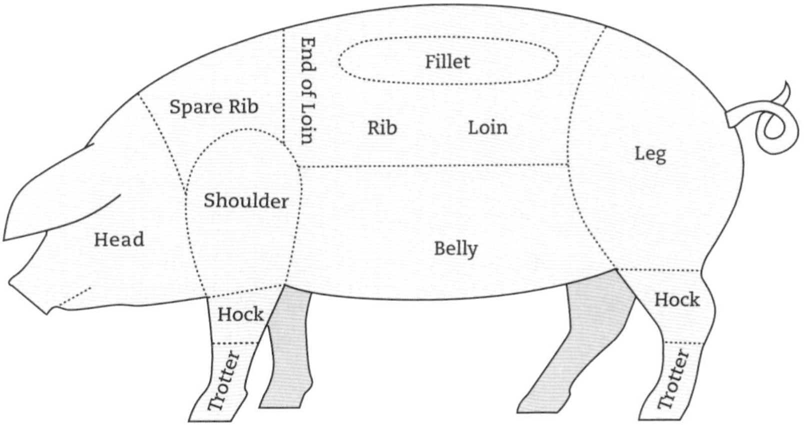

End of Loin · Fillet · Spare Rib · Rib · Loin · Leg · Shoulder · Head · Belly · Hock · Hock · Trotter · Trotter

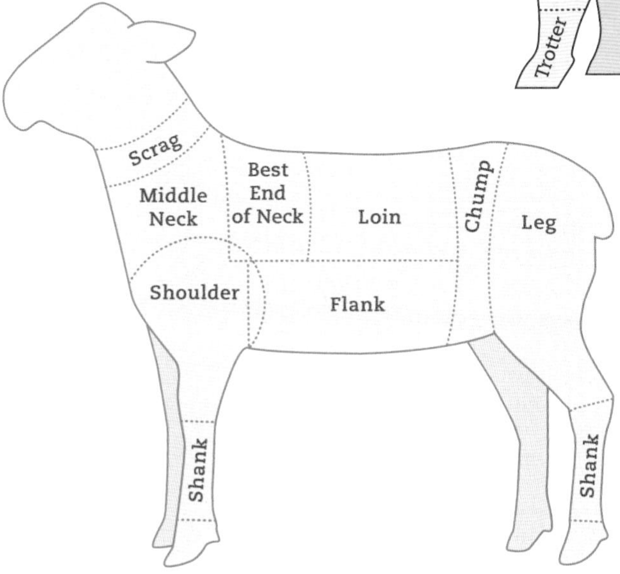

Lamb

Scrag · Best End of Neck · Chump · Middle Neck · Loin · Leg · Shoulder · Flank · Shank · Shank (although some meat that is still classed as game may now be farmed). Venison is dark red and looks firm. Game birds, such as grouse, partridge, pheasant, pigeon and quail are best eaten young when they will be at their most tender. If buying whole birds, look at the legs to check they look smooth as this is an indication that they are still young.

All meat should be kept chilled. Store it on the bottom shelf of the fridge, on a plate or in a container to make sure no blood drips on any other ingredient.

BEEF CUTS

Shin comes from the bottom of the leg on a cow and can be bought on or off the bone. It is a tough cut and can look quite sinewy; because of this, it needs to be cooked slowly over a long period.

Oxtail is the end of the tail and has a single piece of bone in the middle with the flesh of the meat surrounding it. Again, long slow cooking is required here. It is an inexpensive cut, produces rich results and because of this is ideal in stews and soups where a little can go a long way.

Chuck, also known as chuck steak, comes from the shoulder of the animal. It's a tough cut that requires long, slow cooking and is therefore ideal for braising (see page 23) – because of this it is also known as braising steak. It is also ground up and used for minced beef because of its balance of meat to fat ratio and its depth of flavour.

Middle rib is the next cut of meat along the shoulder from chuck, but can be slightly more fatty. It's best to slow-roast it or cut it into bite-sized pieces and make it into a stew.

Forerib, also called rib of beef, is known as one of the prime cuts because it is very tender and flavoursome, too. It's a majestic cut attached to the bone, holding a good portion of meat. The meat is covered in a generous layer of fat and is marbled throughout, too. When the joint is roasted, the fat helps to baste the meat and flavour it. When planning how much to buy, one rib will hold enough meat to serve two people, so work upwards from that. Seal the meat by browning in a hot pan with a little oil first, then roast in a medium oven. If the joint is prepared without the bone ('off the bone'), your butcher will have rolled it into a joint ready to roast in the oven.

Wing rib is the part of the animal that is also known as rib of beef (along with fore rib, above). It has a thin covering of fat around the meat and can be roasted on or off the bone.

Sirloin is the cut that sits between the forerib and rump on the back of the cow, and is an excellent roasting joint. With its layer of fat surrounding the meat, it becomes beautifully tender after roasting. Sirloin steaks can be cut from the fore rib, wing rib and upper sirloin and are slightly pricier than rump steak or minute steak (see below). They have a thin edge of fat and marbling throughout, which helps to flavour the finished dish.

Rump comes from the back of a cow, between the sirloin and topside, and is a tender cut. It is a large steak, which can be either grilled or fried. One whole steak can serve two people, so to share it after cooking slice across the grain into thin ribbon-like pieces. Alternatively, remove the fat and slice thinly before cooking and stir-fry in a hot pan until just cooked.

Fillet, which is butchered from the sirloin and a little part of the rump, is a lean cut, containing very little fat. It is a tender cut so cooks quickly if sliced into steaks (tournedos). It can be pan-fried or roasted whole, but it is pricey so isn't economical for a large number of people.

Thin flank, from the belly of the cow, is a quick-cook cut and can be marinated beforehand to ensure it's tender after cooking. Slice thinly and pan-fry for a minute in a hot pan, or cut into strips and stir-fry.

Thick flank, from the hindquarters of the cow, is sold either rolled and tied up into a joint or cut into pieces. It is a tough cut so is good for braising to make it tender. It can also be sliced into minute steaks, so called because they're cut so thinly that they can be pan-fried in a minute.

Topside is the joint butchered from the top of the back leg of a cow. It is a lean cut and, because it contains very little fat in the meat, it is good roasted medium–rare, so slices will still be tender and have the most flavour. It's a neat, boneless joint, which makes it easy to carve and is cheaper than the other roasting joints such as sirloin, rib of beef or fillet.

Silverside joins topside the other side of the rump at the back leg of the cow, and is good for braising, stewing and pot-roasting. As it is a very lean cut, it needs to be basted regularly so that the meat doesn't end up tasting dry.

LAMB CUTS

Scrag is the top of the neck of the lamb and is very bony with less meat on it. It is a cheap cut and very flavoursome but requires long, slow cooking so is ideal in a stew.

Middle neck, also called lamb neck, is the joint next to scrag and has ribbons of fat running through it. It is a tough cut so is best slow-cooked. Braise it in a stew over a low heat for the best flavour, leaving it really tender. New season's middle neck, from a younger animal, is much more tender, so this can also be marinated (oil, garlic and lemon are great) and cooked over a much more intense heat for less time, which will still produce a tender dish.

Best end of neck, or neck fillet, is the first six to eight bones of the neck and can be prepared on or off the bone. On the bone it is also called rack of lamb. A rack can be cut into single cutlets, which can be grilled or pan-fried until just pink in the middle. The fillet can also be taken off the bone for a cannon of lamb (ask your butcher to do this for you to ensure you get the most meat from the bones). Pan-fry this neat roll of meat first to brown it, then roast it quickly in a hot oven until just pink in the middle. The rack can also be prepared French-trimmed, a term that means using a small sharp knife to clean away all the fat from the bones and remove most of the fat from the meat, leaving just a thin layer behind. This can be roasted as it is, simply seasoned, but the classic way is to add extra flavour to the thin layer of fat by rubbing it with mustard and coating it with breadcrumbs and herbs.

Shoulder, from the front leg of the lamb, is an ideal roasting joint (either on the bone or taken off and stuffed) as it cooks until tender. It's fattier than a leg of lamb and for this reason it is also good slow-roasted so the meat can be pulled easily away from the bone and just melts in the mouth.

Leg is perfect for roasting on the bone, too, as this gives it the most flavour. The bone acts as a conductor of heat, which helps roast the meat from the inside outwards, which in turn maximises the taste. The bone also contains marrow, which imparts its unique flavour to the meat. The meat inside the leg is lean, with an outer layer of thin fat, which helps to baste the meat, leaving it deliciously tender. The leg can be braised for a long time over a low heat until the meat is so tender it can be pulled off the bone into shreds.

Loin is butchered from the middle back of the animal and can be cut into chops. This meat, when cooked, is very tender. Although chops can be cooked quickly, they can also be slowly braised for several hours in a low oven or in a lidded casserole with vegetables and stock until the meat pulls away from the bone easily. The loin can also be prepared without the bone, rolled into a joint. With its generous layer of fat and lean roll of meat inside, it is perfect for roasting.

Flank or breast of lamb is from the belly of the lamb. It is a very fatty cut of meat, but because of this is very economical. It is best stuffed and roasted until the fat softens and some of it melts away.

Chump is from the backside between the leg and lower back of the sheep (the equivalent cut on a cow is the rump). It is a thick piece of meat with an even layer of fat and is mainly prepared into chops and steaks. It can be pan-fried or griddled or marinated and cooked over the coals of a barbecue.

Shank is from the ankle of the animal. The flesh of the meat clings around a central bone and is covered with a layer of fat. It is quite tough so requires long, slow cooking and is often braised with lots of vegetables, canned tomatoes and wine for a delicious one-pot supper.

PORK CUTS

Head is not an everyday cut but it is the main ingredient, along with pigs' trotters and tail, for brawn, the pork-rich terrine set in jelly. It needs to be cooked in a pan of simmering water until tender for this recipe, then the stock becomes gelatinous and is used to set the meat into the terrine.

Hock is between the trotter and the shoulder or leg. It is a tough cut and needs to be braised for a long time until tender. It comes with the bone in and is therefore full of flavour. It is best used in soups and stews and is also an ideal cut for smoking, as this process both tenderises and flavours the meat.

Shoulder is an inexpensive boneless cut that becomes deliciously tender if it is slow-roasted. It also has a thick layer of fat on it, so while the meat is cooking, the outside will crisp up and turn into crackling (see TIP opposite). The cut can also be sliced into steaks with the fat removed.

Trotters have a gelatinous consistency so are good for making stocks. The hind trotters have another culinary benefit: they are longer than the front trotters so can be stuffed with meat or a savoury mousse and cooked until tender. They are also more tender as pigs put more weight on their shoulders as they root for food, so they don't work as hard as the front trotters.

Spare ribs are sold either individually or as a rack. They're the bones left over after the meat has been cut away and even though the meat on them is sparse, they're still very tasty. They're a tough cut so need to be simmered first to tenderise the meat, then covered in a marinade to flavour them and roasted in the oven to intensify this.

Belly, from the stomach of the pig, has thick layers of fat in between the meat, making it a delicious roasting joint. It is also good braised, so the fat melts away and leaves the meat very tender. For braises, however, it is best to remove the top layer of fat before cooking so the finished dish doesn't end up swimming in a layer of grease.

Loin is an ideal roasting joint, either on or off the bone. When it is boned and rolled, the joint is easy to carve but it is a lean cut so take care not to overcook it otherwise it will become dry. The layer of skin on the outside produces really crisp crackling, too (see TIP opposite). It can also be stuffed with a savoury stuffing.

Tenderloin is from the fillet of the loin. It's a long, thin piece of lean meat, with very little fat (so there's no crackling). Because of this it is ideal for quick-cooking, and can be cubed, sliced or cut into thin pieces for stir-frying. It can also be roasted for a short time, but because it has very little fat, benefits from being marinated with oil, garlic, lemon and spices or wrapped in bacon for extra flavour.

Leg is good for roasting. It's a lean cut with fat on the outside, so the roasting brings out the flavour, leaving the meat still tender. The thickest part of the leg is called the chump, and this part can be butchered and sold as steaks or chops.

TIP

To make great crackling on any of the roasting joints above, remove the wrapping from the meat and place the joint on a plate. Pat the skin dry with kitchen paper, then score it all over with a sharp knife or scalpel. Rub in salt just before cooking. After the joint has finished roasting, if all the skin hasn't crisped up, remove it from the meat using a sharp knife. Place under a preheated grill, watching it carefully, until has become crispy.

Making the Most of the Freezer

Stocking your freezer with a good variety of ingredients and homemade meals is a great way of always having supper to hand. Make sure you wrap up the food well and that it's airtight, either in freezerproof containers (which are preferable as they can be reused) or in plastic film, so there's no chance of the contents unwrapping and getting freezer burn. This is where the top of the food hasn't been covered properly so the air has got to it. It looks like it is covered in a light frosting of ice or it may appear bruised. It doesn't affect the flavour of the food, but it may spoil the appearance and it may dry it out a little. Label and mark all items with the date.

It is also important to pack your freezer until it's full, as it is more economical to run this way. Remember to go through the drawers regularly to check what's stored inside, or write down the contents of each drawer, so that food gets used up often and in rotation and nothing gets wasted.

Whole fish should be scaled and gutted and can be frozen on the day of purchase, the same as fillets, for up to six weeks.

Poultry can be frozen for up to three months on the day of purchase, and the same applies to game. For lamb, beef and pork, freeze on the day of purchase for up to six months.

Summer fruit freezes well: open freeze first on a tray, then bag or box up. Hard fruit should be poached first before freezing. Freeze both for up to six months.

Most fresh vegetables do not freeze well unless they have been blanched first, are simmered to a purée or have been cooked in a sauce. Freeze for up to six months.

Fresh herbs freeze well. Chop finely and spoon into ice cube trays. Drizzle over water to cover and freeze. To use, they can be popped straight out of the ice cube trays from frozen and stirred into soups and stews at the end of cooking.

Other ingredients that freeze well are: bread and cake (up to six months); egg yolks (beaten with a pinch of sugar to be used in sweet recipes or with a pinch of salt for savoury dishes) and egg whites (for meringues) – both for up to six months; double cream – whipped before freezing; and skimmed and semi-skimmed milk, which can be frozen for up to three months.

There are several methods of thawing food. If you're organised, take the raw ingredient or cooked dish out of the freezer and leave at cool room temperature overnight to thaw gradually. This is best for baked and cooked dishes. Alternatively, you can thaw food in a microwave on the lowest setting – this is fine for soups, stews and bread. However, depending on your model, it may mean that parts of the food thaw quicker than others, so when you come to cook them they start to cook quicker. It's best therefore to remove the food from the microwave every minute or so and stir it so that it thaws evenly.

Small raw ingredients that need thawing quickly, such as frozen prawns, can be thawed under cold running water.

A NOTE ON USE-BY AND BEST-BEFORE DATES

Use-by dates are the dates that are marked on fresh food, such as meat, fish, milk and yoghurts, indicating the time before which you must consume the product. The food will go off if not eaten before that time.

Best-before dates are placed on food that tastes best before that date. Depending on how you store this food, it can sometimes be eaten after that date.

Soup

Spiced Tomato Soup

PREPARATION TIME: 15 MINS | COOKING TIME: 45–55 MINS | SERVES 6 | ❄

This spicy soup is made using a combination of fresh and canned tomatoes. When they are in season, use the ripest fresh ones you can find with a good deep red colour. This is when tomatoes are at their sweetest and most flavoursome and will make this a spectacular soup.

3 tbsp sunflower oil
2 onions, roughly
    chopped
3 carrots, roughly
    chopped
2 garlic cloves, crushed
500g Sainsbury's flavour
    ripe tomatoes,
    chopped
1 tbsp paprika
1 tbsp coriander seeds,
    crushed
1 tbsp cumin seeds,
    crushed
1 tsp granulated or
    caster sugar
800g Sainsbury's
    canned chopped
    tomatoes,
300ml hot Sainsbury's
    Signature vegetable
    stock
sea salt and freshly
    ground black pepper
chopped fresh coriander,
    to garnish
mini poppadoms, to
    serve

HEAT THE OIL in a large pan over a high heat and cook the onions, carrots and garlic for 10–15 minutes until the onions have softened and are just beginning to turn golden.

ADD THE FRESH TOMATOES with the paprika, crushed coriander and cumin seeds and cook over a medium heat for 3 minutes until deliciously aromatic. Season well and stir in the sugar.

POUR OVER THE CANNED TOMATOES and stock (you may not need all of the stock, depending on how watery the tomatoes are), then bring to the boil and cook for 30–40 minutes.

SERVE GARNISHED with the chopped fresh coriander and with the poppadoms alongside.

44

SOUP

PER SERVING
128 cals
6.1g fat
0.8g saturated fat
12g total sugars
0.3g salt

TIP
To serve this as a simple, prepare-ahead dinner party dish, garnish with finely chopped cucumber and spring onions.

Leek and Potato Soup

PREPARATION TIME: 10 MINS | COOKING TIME: 15 MINS | SERVES 4 | ❄

This most satisfying soup requires only two cooking stages. The potatoes and garlic are simmered in stock first, to flavour, then mashed into the cooking liquor. Use the best olive oil you can for the vital finishing splash of flavour.

575g Sainsbury's Taste
    The Difference Vivaldi
    potatoes (or
    alternative floury
    potatoes)
2–3 garlic cloves
1.2 litres Sainsbury's
    Signature vegetable
    stock
350g leeks, trimmed
celery salt (optional)
4 tbsp roughly chopped
    fresh parsley
4 tsp extra virgin
    olive oil
salt and freshly
    ground pepper
crusty bread, to serve

PER SERVING
220 cals
3.7g fat
0.5g saturated fat
2.7g total sugars
0.8g salt

PEEL AND THINLY SLICE the potatoes and garlic. Place in a saucepan with the stock. Bring to the boil and add salt. Cover and simmer for about 10 minutes until the potatoes are soft.

MEANWHILE, SLICE THE LEEKS. Add them to the potatoes and simmer for a further 5 minutes or so to soften them.

ROUGHLY MASH THE POTATOES into the liquid, using a potato masher. Adjust the seasoning with celery salt (if using) or plain salt and pepper to taste. Stir in the chopped parsley.

LADLE THE SOUP into warmed bowls and drizzle 1 teaspoon of olive oil over each serving. Serve immediately, with chunks ofcrusty bread.

VARIATION

Use roughly chopped watercress instead of parsley.

TIP

Don't be tempted to use a food processor or blender to mash potatoes as it will make the texture gluey.

Pea and Ham Soup

PREPARATION TIME: 15 MINS *plus overnight soaking* | COOKING TIME: 1¾ HOURS |
SERVES 8 *as a starter* | ❄

A meaty gammon joint, given long gentle simmering, makes a
deliciously rich base for this well-loved, robust soup. Spoonfuls of crème
fraîche, added to each serving, provide a refreshing contrast and make
the soup taste so much more special. Don't forget to soften the dried
green peas by soaking overnight, then rinse them well before cooking
with the meat. As a warming wintry main course, accompanied by
plenty of crusty bread, this soup will serve four.

450g dried split or whole
   green peas
1–1.1kg Sainsbury's
   smoked or unsmoked
   gammon joint
2 large onions, roughly
   chopped
2 carrots, roughly sliced
2 celery sticks, cut into
   chunks
2 bay leaves
150ml Sainsbury's half
   fat crème fraîche
salt and freshly ground
   black pepper
fresh parsley leaves,
   to garnish

PER SERVING
407 cals
13.7g fat
5.1g saturated fat
4.9g total sugars
3.4g salt

PUT THE DRIED PEAS IN A LARGE BOWL and cover with
plenty of cold water. Leave to soak overnight.

PLACE THE GAMMON IN A LARGE SAUCEPAN and cover with
cold water. Bring slowly to the boil, then drain and return to
the clean pan. Drain the peas and add to the pan.

ADD THE ONIONS, CARROTS, CELERY AND BAY LEAVES
to the pan. Cover with cold water and bring to the boil.

REDUCE THE HEAT AND COVER THE PAN WITH A LID.
Simmer very gently for 1½ hours until the bacon and peas
are very tender. Discard the bay leaves.

LIFT THE GAMMON FROM THE PAN. Cut into chunks, then
chop finely.

PURÉE THE SOUP IN A BLENDER or food processor until
smooth, then place in a clean pan with the chopped meat.
Heat through gently, adding a little stock if the soup is very
thick. Season with a little salt and pepper, if necessary.

LADLE THE SOUP INTO WARMED BOWLS and add a generous
spoonful of crème fraîche to each one. Serve garnished with
roughly torn parsley.

49

SOUP

TIP
Using a blender rather
than a food processor for
puréeing the soup gives a
smoother result.

VARIATION

Use yellow split peas instead of green
ones, cooking them in the same way.

Tuscan Bean and Rosemary Soup

PREPARATION TIME: 15 MINS | COOKING TIME: 50 MINS | SERVES 6 | ❄

This is a typical staple dish from Italy – a long, slow-cooked hearty broth that can sustain until the next meal or be the first of several courses. To serve it as the Italians would, place some crusty bread in the bottom of individual bowls and ladle the soup over the top.

4 garlic cloves
8 tbsp roughly chopped By Sainsbury's fresh rosemary
6 tbsp olive oil
2 celery sticks, roughly chopped
2 carrots, roughly chopped
2 onions, roughly chopped
1 tbsp tomato purée
400g can chopped tomatoes
1.5 litres vegetable stock
3 x 400g Sainsbury's cans haricot beans, rinsed and drained
½ Savoy cabbage or 2 heads of greens, finely sliced
salt and freshly ground black pepper
crusty bread, to serve
extra virgin olive oil to serve

PLACE THE GARLIC, ROSEMARY AND A LARGE PINCH OF SALT on a chopping board and chop until fine. Using the flat of the blade, crush to release the rosemary oils.

HEAT THE OLIVE OIL IN A LARGE SAUCEPAN over a medium heat and cook the celery, carrots, onions, garlic, rosemary and plenty of freshly ground pepper for 10 minutes until softened.

ADD THE TOMATO PURÉE, chopped tomatoes, stock and beans. Cover and bring to a simmer. Cook for 40 minutes, adding the cabbage or greens for the last 15 minutes of cooking. Serve in warmed bowls drizzled with extra virgin olive oil.

VARIATION
This can also be made with kidney beans or cannellini beans.

PER SERVING
329 cals
12.1g fat
1.7g saturated fat
12.9g total sugars
2g salt

Hot and Sour Soup

PREPARATION TIME: 15 MINS | COOKING TIME: 25 MINS | SERVES 4

Traditionally, the pungent Thai flavours in this soup are not removed before serving but they are not meant to be eaten.

1 stick By Sainsbury's lemon grass
1 or 2 red chillies
2 garlic cloves, thinly sliced
2.5cm piece fresh root ginger, thinly sliced
handful of fresh coriander sprigs
1.2 litres Sainsbury's Signature chicken stock
1 chicken breast fillet, skinned
125g mushrooms, preferably shiitake or baby button mushrooms, halved or sliced if large
juice of 2 limes
about 2 tbsp light soy sauce
1–2 spring onions, to garnish

PER SERVING
115 cals
0.6g fat
0.1g saturated fat
0.8g total sugars
2.2g salt

CRUSH THE LEMON GRASS using a rolling pin and place in a large saucepan. Slice 1 or 2 chillies (retaining the seeds), depending on how hot you like your soup – but it should be fairly hot. Add the chillies, garlic and ginger to the pan with half the coriander and all the stock. Cover and bring to the boil.

WHEN THE STOCK HAS COME TO THE BOIL, reduce the heat so that it is just simmering. Drop the chicken breast and mushrooms into the soup. Cover and simmer gently for 20 minutes until the chicken is cooked through.

MEANWHILE, MAKE THE GARNISH. Trim the spring onions and cut into 8cm lengths. Halve each piece lengthways, then cut into very fine shreds. Drop them into a bowl of cold water and leave in the refrigerator to curl (this garnish is not essential; if you're short of time you could simply trim the spring onions and cut into thin slices on the diagonal).

CHECK THAT THE CHICKEN IS COOKED then shred it roughly and return it to the pan. Add the lime juice and soy sauce to the soup, then taste. The flavour should be fairly hot and faintly sour. If it needs more salt, add a little extra soy sauce. Add more chilli if necessary. Remove and discard the coriander sprigs.

DRAIN THE CURLED SPRING ONION SHREDS. Ladle the soup into warmed bowls and top each with a pile of onion shreds and the remaining coriander sprigs.

VARIATION

Replace the chicken with 225g peeled raw prawns. Simmer the soup with the mushrooms for 20 minutes before adding the prawns. Add the prawns and simmer gently for 4–5 minutes or until the prawns are cooked through (they will look pink and opaque).

TIP

For a more substantial soup to serve as a lunch or light supper, add some fine egg noodles 5 minutes before the end of the cooking time.

Carrot and Coriander Soup

PREPARATION TIME: 15 MINS | COOKING TIME: 35 MINS | SERVES 6 | ❄

This classic combination of flavours – the earthy sweetness of carrots and subtle hint of spice – is a real crowd-pleaser. Serve with plenty of fresh crusty bread.

15g butter
1 tbsp vegetable oil
1 onion, finely chopped
1 celery stick, chopped
1 small garlic clove, chopped
2 tsp By Sainsbury's ground coriander
800g By Sainsbury's carrots, cut into 2cm slices
1.2 litres hot Sainsbury's Signature chicken or vegetable stock
1 tbsp chopped By Sainsbury's fresh coriander, plus extra sprigs to garnish
juice of ¼ lemon
salt and freshly ground black pepper

MELT THE BUTTER WITH THE OIL in a pan over a medium heat. As soon as the butter stops foaming, add the onion and celery and cook, covered with a lid, for 10–15 minutes until softened. Stir in the garlic and ground coriander and cook for 1–2 minutes.

STIR IN THE CARROTS, season with salt and pepper, add the hot stock and cover. Bring up to the boil and simmer for 20 minutes until the carrots are tender.

COOL A LITTLE, then add the chopped coriander and purée until smooth.

RETURN TO THE PAN AND REHEAT GENTLY, adding a little more water if the soup is too thick. Stir in the lemon juice and season again, then ladle into bowls and garnish with the coriander sprigs.

PER SERVING
132 cals
4.3g fat
1.6g saturated fat
10.3g total sugars
0.6g salt

TIP

This soup freezes beautifully. Pour into a container and allow to cool, then seal and freeze for up to three months. Cool overnight at cool room temperature and reheat in a pan until thoroughly heated through.

Tomato and Vegetable Soup

PREPARATION TIME: 30 MINS, *plus overnight soaking* | COOKING TIME: 1¾ HOURS |
SERVES 6–8

This colourful vegetable soup from Provence is lifted with the sunny flavours of garlic, basil and golden olive oil pounded together to a *pistou* or paste similar to the Italian pesto. The soup is delicious reheated and eaten the next day once the flavours have had time to meld. The variations are endless – simply use whatever vegetables are in season.

125g Sainsbury's dried black-eyed beans (or dried haricot or navy beans)
450g ripe tomatoes
3 tbsp olive oil
1 onion, sliced
1 leek, sliced
2 carrots, diced
175g potatoes, diced
a few fresh thyme sprigs
2 bay leaves
125g green beans, roughly chopped
350g courgettes, diced
125g By Sainsbury's fresh or frozen peas (optional)
75g Sainsbury's dried vermicelli
salt and freshly ground black pepper

For the pistou
25g By Sainsbury's basil leaves
4 garlic cloves
150ml extra virgin olive oil

PER SERVING
308 cals
19.1g fat
2.9g saturated fat
6.5g total sugars
trace salt

PLACE THE BEANS IN A BOWL, cover with plenty of cold water and leave to soak overnight. The next day, drain the beans and transfer to a large pan. Cover with cold water and bring to the boil. Boil steadily for 10 minutes, then lower the heat, cover and simmer for about 45 minutes to 1 hour until almost tender. Drain.

PUT THE TOMATOES IN A BOWL, cover with boiling water and leave for 30 seconds. Drain well, return the tomatoes to the bowl and cover with cold water. Peel away the skins and dice the flesh.

HEAT THE OIL IN A LARGE PAN, add the onion and leek and cook gently for 10 minutes until beginning to soften. Add the cooked dried beans, carrots, potatoes and herbs. Pour in enough water to cover – about 1.2 litres. Bring to the boil, cover and simmer for 30 minutes until the white beans begin to disintegrate.

MEANWHILE, MAKE THE PISTOU. Pound the basil and garlic in a pestle and mortar until paste-like, then gradually work in the olive oil until amalgamated. Add salt and pepper to taste.

ADD THE GREEN BEANS, courgettes, peas (if using), tomatoes and vermicelli to the soup. Season with salt and pepper. Cook for a further 10–15 minutes until all the vegetables and pasta are very tender. Check the seasoning.

SPOON A LITTLE PISTOU INTO THE SOUP TO FLAVOUR, then ladle into warmed bowls and serve piping hot, offering extra *pistou* separately.

> **TIP**
> If you don't have a pestle and mortar, make the *pistou* in a food processor. Whizz the garlic and basil together first, then drizzle in the olive oil through the feeder tube. Any leftovers can be frozen in portions and used to flavour other vegetable soups or drizzled over vegetable pasta dishes with freshly grated Parmesan.

Butternut Squash and White Bean Soup

PREPARATION TIME: 15 MINS | COOKING TIME: 40 MINS | SERVES 6 | ❄ *(without garnish)*

Rich and sweet, butternut squash is a perfect base for a warming autumnal soup. Here it's combined with red pepper and white beans, which gives the soup a creamy finish. When in season, the butternut squash can also be replaced with pumpkin.

1 red pepper, deseeded

1kg By Sainsbury's butternut squash, deseeded

3 tbsp olive oil, plus a little extra for frying

1 large onion, roughly chopped

2 garlic cloves, finely chopped

400g can cannellini beans, drained

1 tsp cayenne pepper

1 litre Sainsbury's Signature vegetable stock

75g chorizo, diced into small pieces

salt and freshly ground black pepper

PER SERVING

284 cals

10.8g fat

2.3g saturated fat

13.5g total sugars

0.7g salt

ROUGHLY CHOP THE PEPPERS AND SQUASH, reserving a quarter of the pepper and about 100g of the squash. Heat the olive oil over a medium heat in a large pan. Add the chopped pepper and squash, onion and garlic and cover with a lid. Allow to cook gently for 10 minutes.

ADD THE CANNELINI BEANS, cayenne pepper and stock. Stir together and season with salt and pepper. Cover, bring to the boil then turn down the heat to low and cook for 30 minutes, until the vegetables are tender. Cool a little then whizz in a blender or food processor until smooth. Return the soup to the pan.

ABOUT 15 MINUTES BEFORE THE END OF THE COOKING TIME, heat 1 teaspoon of olive oil in a small frying pan, add the diced chorizo and the reserved chopped pepper and squash and cook for 10 minutes, over a medium heat, stirring until the squash is golden.

TO SERVE, REHEAT THE SOUP GENTLY AND check the seasoning. Ladle the soup into warmed bowls then top with the chorizo and vegetable garnish.

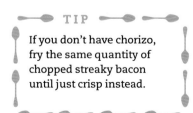

TIP

If you don't have chorizo, fry the same quantity of chopped streaky bacon until just crisp instead.

Broccoli and Stilton Soup

PREPARATION TIME: 15 MINS | COOKING TIME: 15–20 MINS | SERVES 4 | ❄

The addition of blue cheese to this soup is very subtle so as not to overpower the flavour of the broccoli. The recipe calls for the whole head of broccoli – root and florets – so is economical, too.

25g butter
1 bunch spring onions, roughly chopped
1 head of broccoli, about 275g
900ml hot Sainsbury's Signature vegetable stock
50g Sainsbury's blue Stilton, crumbled, plus extra to serve
salt and freshly ground black pepper
1 tbsp chopped chives, to garnish

MELT THE BUTTER IN A PAN over a medium heat. When the butter stops foaming, add the spring onions and cook gently for 5 minutes until softened.

CHOP THE BROCCOLI, including the stalk, and add to the pan. Season well and toss to coat in the buttery juices. Add the vegetable stock, cover and simmer for 10–15 minutes.

ALLOW THE SOUP TO COOL A LITTLE then blend until smooth. Stir in the crumbled Stilton and season again.

LADLE INTO FOUR BOWLS, then garnish with extra Stilton, the chives and a pinch of black pepper.

PER SERVING
176 cals
10.3g fat
6.3g saturated fat
1.7g total sugars
0.99g salt

TIP

This soup makes an ideal starter, and will stretch to serving six if you top it with some black pepper and garlic croutons. Cut three thick slices of bread into cubes. Mix together 1 crushed garlic clove with 1 tablespoon of olive oil and a good pinch of freshly ground black pepper. Brush all over the cubes of bread and bake in the oven at 200°C/180°Fan/Mark 6 for 5–10 minutes until golden.

Moroccan Chickpea Soup

PREPARATION TIME: 15 MINS | COOKING TIME: 30 MINS | SERVES 4 | ❄

This soup is tasty and packed with goodness. It is good for a British summer – when gazpacho is too cold, but a heavier soup is not right either.

2 tbsp olive oil

2 onions, roughly chopped

2 garlic cloves, crushed

2 carrots, roughly chopped

1 tsp By Sainsbury's paprika

1 tbsp By Sainsbury's cumin seeds

1 red pepper, roughly chopped

800ml hot Sainsbury's Signature vegetable stock

2 x 400g cans chopped tomatoes

2 x 400g cans Sainsbury's chickpeas, drained and rinsed

salt and freshly ground black pepper

50g mixed seeds, toasted, to garnish

4 tbsp chopped fresh coriander, to garnish

HEAT THE OLIVE OIL IN A LARGE SAUCEPAN over a medium heat and cook the onions, garlic and carrots for a few minutes until softened. Stir in the paprika and cumin and cook for a further 3 minutes or so until the cumin smells aromatic.

STIR IN THE RED PEPPER and add the stock and the canned tomatoes and chickpeas. Season well with salt and pepper. Cover and cook for 30 minutes until the pepper is tender.

WHEN READY TO EAT, take half of the soup out of the pan and blend the remainder. Return the unblended half to the pan and give it a good stir. This gives the soup some texture, but it is, of course, optional – you can blend all of it.

SERVE THE SOUP GARNISHED with the toasted seeds and chopped fresh coriander.

PER SERVING

388 cals

15.4g fat

2.1g saturated fat

14.3g total sugars

1.5g salt

TIP

For an easy lunch, serve the soup with toasted pitta bread, cut into fingers, and a pot of hummus for dipping.

63

SOUP

Corn Chowder

PREPARATION TIME: 15 MINS | COOKING TIME: 1 HOUR | SERVES 6

Late summer is the prime season for corn on the cob. Its flavour is so sweet, you can also eat the kernels raw, stripped straight from their thick stem (see TIP). Corn cobs are cheap and widely available during this time, and require very little cooking. Add them right at the end of this creamy rich soup, so they provide a little bit of texture to the finished dish.

60g butter
2 onions, chopped
1 red pepper, deseeded and chopped
4 rashers Sainsbury's Taste The Difference Wiltshire Cured Ultimate unsmoked back bacon, chopped
4 new potatoes, diced
2 beef tomatoes, chopped
1 litre Sainsbury's Signature chicken stock
4 corn cobs
150ml Sainsbury's double cream
150ml hot Sainsbury's Signature vegetable stock
salt and freshly ground black pepper

PER SERVING
352 cals
21.8g fat
12.2g saturated fat
6.1g total sugars
1.3g salt

HEAT THE BUTTER IN A LARGE PAN over a medium heat and cook the onions, red pepper and bacon for 5–10 minutes, until beginning to soften. Season with pepper.

STIR IN THE POTATOES, tomatoes and chicken stock. Check the seasoning and then leave to cook for 30–40 minutes until the vegetables are tender.

MEANWHILE, REMOVE THE KERNELS FROM THE CORN COBS (see TIP). About 15 minutes before the end of the cooking time, stir in the corn kernels into the pan. Cook for 10 minutes, then stir in the double cream and stock and heat through. Serve hot.

TIP

To remove the kernels from the cob, hold the cobs, one at a time, inside a clean plastic bag. Take a sharp knife and run it straight down between the rows of corn, cutting away from you. The kernels will collect in the bag rather than flying all over your kitchen.

Bouillabaisse

PREPARATION TIME: 15 MINS | COOKING TIME: 1 HOUR | SERVES 4-6

The most famous of all Mediterranean fish soups, this colourful combination of fish and shellfish in a flavourful broth originated in Marseilles. Some of the fish included in the authentic version are unavailable in this country but it is possible to create a delicious dish using alternatives. Serve with plenty of crusty bread.

1.5kg mixed fish and shellfish, such as mullet, John Dory, monkfish, red snapper, whiting, large prawns, mussels
225g plum tomatoes (or other well-flavoured tomatoes)
pinch of By Sainsbury's saffron strands
50ml olive oil
1 onion, sliced
1 leek, trimmed and sliced
1 celery stick, diced
2 garlic cloves, crushed
1 bouquet garni
1 strip of orange peel
½ tsp By Sainsbury's fennel seeds
1 tbsp sun-dried tomato paste
2 tsp Pernod
2–3 tbsp chopped parsley
salt and freshly ground black pepper

PER SERVING
241 cals
7.9g fat
1.2g saturated fat
2.8g total sugars
0.5g salt

CUT THE HEADS, TAILS AND FINS OFF THE FISH and put them in a pan with 1.2 litres of water. Bring to the boil and simmer for 15 minutes. Strain and reserve the stock.

CUT THE FISH INTO LARGE CHUNKS, but leave shellfish in their shells.

IMMERSE THE TOMATOES IN A BOWL OF BOILING WATER for 30 seconds, then drain and refresh under cold running water. Peel away the skins. Soak the saffron strands in 1–2 tablespoons of boiling water.

HEAT THE OIL IN A LARGE PAN, add the onion, leek and celery and cook until softened. Add the tomatoes, garlic, bouquet garni, orange peel and fennel seeds. Add the saffron with its soaking liquid, and the reserved fish stock. Season with salt and pepper, bring to the boil and simmer for 30–40 minutes.

ADD THE SHELLFISH AND SIMMER FOR ABOUT 6 MINUTES. Add the fish and cook for a further 6–8 minutes until it flakes easily. If necessary, add a little water to ensure there is enough liquid to cover the fish.

USING A SLOTTED SPOON, transfer the fish to a warmed serving platter. Keep the liquid boiling to allow the oil to emulsify with the broth. Add the sundried tomato paste and Pernod and check the seasoning. Return the fish to the broth, sprinkle with the parsley and serve.

67

SOUP

TIP
Croutons can be served with the broth. To make these, fry small chunks of bread in olive oil until golden and crisp, drain well on kitchen paper, then sprinkle lightly with salt.

Fish & Seafood

Mediterranean Cod and Olive Stew

PREPARATION TIME: 15 MINS | COOKING TIME: 35 MINS | SERVES 4

This full-flavoured stew makes an easy midweek supper or a simple yet impressive dinner-party dish. Serve with long-grain and wild rice or with buttered new potatoes.

2 tbsp olive oil
2 onions, roughly chopped
1 carrot, roughly chopped
1 red pepper, roughly chopped
3 garlic cloves, crushed
1 tbsp fennel seeds, crushed
400g can chopped tomatoes
200ml white wine
4 x 150g pieces of line-caught cod loin
grated zest of 1 lemon
4 tbsp finely chopped flat-leaf parsley
75g Sainsbury's rustic chopped natural black olives in brine, drained
salt and freshly ground black pepper

HEAT THE OIL IN A LARGE, LIDDED FLAMEPROOF CASSEROLE PAN over a medium heat and cook the onions for 10 minutes until starting to soften.

ADD THE CARROT, PEPPER AND GARLIC and continue to cook for 5 minutes. Stir in the fennel seeds, tomatoes and white wine. Bring to the boil and simmer for 2 minutes to cook off the alcohol.

SEASON THE FISH WITH SALT AND PEPPER and add to the sauce. Cover the pan, bring to the boil, then turn the heat right down low and simmer for about 20 minutes until the fish is cooked all the way through.

JUST BEFORE SERVING, mix together the lemon zest, parsley and black olives and sprinkle over the stew. Serve immediately.

PER SERVING
290 cals
10.1g fat
1.4g saturated fat
9.6g total sugars
0.6g salt

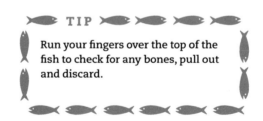

TIP

Run your fingers over the top of the fish to check for any bones, pull out and discard.

Salmon Fillet with Herb Crust

PREPARATION TIME: 15 MINS | COOKING TIME: 20–25 MINS | SERVES 6

A crispy herb and breadcrumb crust flavoured with nuts and nutmeg coats tender salmon fillets. The salmon is cooked skinned-side uppermost to prevent it drying out in the heat of the oven, and the butter in the crust bastes the salmon as it cooks. Serve with a moist accompaniment, such as roasted tomatoes.

1 tbsp mixed peppercorns
6 Sainsbury's responsibly-sourced skinless salmon fillets, each about 175g
150g fresh white breadcrumbs
6 tbsp chopped mixed fresh herbs, such as parsley, tarragon and chervil, plus extra sprigs to garnish
grated zest of 1 orange
¼ tsp By Sainsbury's freshly grated nutmeg
75g Sainsbury's shelled walnuts, chopped
50g butter
1 egg yolk, beaten
salt and freshly ground black pepper

PREHEAT THE OVEN TO 200°C/180°FAN/MARK 6. Crush the peppercorns finely using a pestle and mortar. Rub the pepper evenly over the skinned side of the fish. Place the fish skinned-side uppermost in a shallow baking dish.

MIX THE BREADCRUMBS, herbs, orange zest, nutmeg and walnuts together.

MELT THE BUTTER IN A FRYING PAN and stir in the breadcrumb mixture. Cook over a medium heat until the butter is absorbed and the crumbs are just beginning to brown. Season with salt and pepper.

TURN THE SALMON OVER and brush the skinned side of the salmon with the beaten egg yolk. Coat with the crumb mixture. Place the salmon in one large ovenproof dish or two small dishes. Bake in the preheated oven for 15–20 minutes until the salmon is opaque and the crust is golden and crisp.

TRANSFER THE SALMON FILLETS TO WARMED PLATES. Serve immediately, together with any juices and extra crumbs, garnished with herb sprigs.

FISH & SEAFOOD

PER SERVING
562 cals
36.1g fat
8.9g saturated fat
1g total sugars
0.8g salt

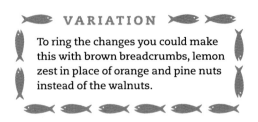

VARIATION

To ring the changes you could make this with brown breadcrumbs, lemon zest in place of orange and pine nuts instead of the walnuts.

Peppered Salmon on a Watercress and Potato Salad

PREPARATION TIME: 15 MINS | COOKING TIME: 20 MINS | SERVES 4

Salmon fillets are encrusted with mixed crushed peppercorns which gives them a crunchy exterior and provides a lovely contrast to the soft salmon flesh, which melts in the mouth.

25g mixed red, green, black and white peppercorns

4 Sainsbury's responsibly-sourced skinless salmon fillets, each about 125g

350g Sainsbury's Taste The Difference Vivaldi new potatoes, halved or quartered if large

150g green beans, trimmed and halved

120ml By Sainsbury's lighter mayonnaise

½ tsp By Sainsbury's Dijon mustard

2 tsp lemon juice

50g watercress, stalks removed, plus extra to garnish

2 tbsp olive oil

freshly ground black pepper

74

PER SERVING
382 cals
22.6g fat
3.2g saturated fat
3g total sugars
0.9g salt

USING A PESTLE AND MORTAR or a spice grinder, roughly grind the peppercorns. Transfer to a shallow dish.

RUN YOUR FINGERS OVER THE SALMON FILLETS to check for any bones and pull out any that may remain using tweezers. Press the salmon filets into the peppercorns to coat the fish thoroughly all over. Cover and set aside.

COOK THE POTATOES IN A LARGE PAN of lightly salted boiling water for 12–15 minutes until tender, adding the green beans for the last 3 minutes. Drain, then refresh briefly under cold running water to stop the cooking process.

MEANWHILE SPOON THE MAYONNAISE into a bowl. Add the mustard, lemon juice and a little pepper and mix well. Chop the watercress and stir into the mayonnaise.

HEAT A HEAVY-BASED FRYING PAN or griddle over a medium–high heat, brush with oil and cook the salmon for for 4–5 minutes on each side, until cooked through.

ARRANGE THE SALMON, potatoes and green beans on a serving platter, garnish with watercress and serve with the mayonnaise.

Asian-style Fish Parcels

PREPARATION TIME: 10 MINS | COOKING TIME: 15-20 MINS | SERVES 6

Steaming fish in a parcel is an easy method of cooking and is very healthy, too. This recipe serves six, so in order to cook six parcels at the same time they are cooked in the oven, but if you're making this for two people, use a steamer instead. Carrots or tenderstem broccoli would work well, too, just make sure they're finely sliced so they will steam and become tender in the cooking time.

500g Thai jasmine rice
1 red pepper, sliced
1 yellow pepper, sliced
150g By Sainsbury's sugar snaps, halved lengthways
1 bulb pak choi or stem of choi sum, roughly chopped
6 Sainsbury's Taste The Difference sea bass fillets, with skin

For the dressing
grated zest and juice of 1 large lime
3 tbsp fish sauce
¼ tsp light muscovado sugar
1 red chilli, finely chopped
1 lemongrass stalk, outer leaves discarded, finely chopped

PER SERVING
480 cals
4.5g fat
1.7g saturated fat
4.4g total sugars
1.3g salt

PREHEAT THE OVEN TO 200°C/180°FAN/MARK 6. Stir all the dressing ingredients together and set aside.

TO PREPARE THE RICE, pour it into a measuring jug and note the volume, then transfer to a medium pan. Add double the volume of boiling water to the rice, cover and bring to a simmer. Turn the heat to its lowest setting and simmer according to the timings on the packet.

CUT OUT SIX SQUARES OF BAKING PARCHMENT, using the length of the roll as a guide. Divide the peppers, sugar snaps and pak choi between them. Skin-side down, roll up the sea bass fillets and put on top of the vegetables.

FOLD ONE HALF OF THE PARCHMENT over the other and wrap up each parcel, twisting the paper together to seal. Leave a gap in the top of each one. Pour about two teaspoons of the dressing into each one through the gap, then seal.

PUT THE PARCELS ON A BAKING SHEET and bake in the oven for 15–20 minutes until the fish is cooked. Check by opening a parcel and gently teasing the flesh of the fish with a fork. If it flakes easily and looks opaque, it's ready.

SERVE THE PARCELS WITH A PORTION OF RICE on the side, and offer any remaining dressing to pour into the parcels.

77

FISH & SEAFOOD

VARIATION

For an alternative dressing, omit the fish sauce and lemongrass and mix together 2 teaspoons of sesame oil, 2 tablespoons of soy sauce, 1 tablespoon of mirin (rice wine) and 2 teaspoons of rice wine vinegar (or white wine vinegar), a 1cm piece of root ginger, cut into matchsticks, and a pinch of salt. Divide among the parcels and cook as above.

Seared Cod with Wilted Spinach

PREPARATION TIME: 35 MINS | COOKING TIME: 15 MINS | SERVES 4

Thick fillets of the freshest cod are quickly pan-fried to crisp the skin, then roasted briefly in the oven until just firm and juicy. Served on a bed of bright green buttery spinach with a creamy, light *beurre blanc* sauce, this is a sophisticated dish, full of contrasting flavours and textures.

4 thick pieces of Sainsbury's Taste The Difference cod loin, with skin, each about 175g
plain flour, for coating
2 tbsp olive oil
900g By Sainsbury's spinach, stalks removed
salt and freshly ground black pepper

For the beurre blanc
2 shallots, finely diced
3 tbsp white wine
3 tbsp Sainsbury's white wine vinegar
1 tbsp double cream
150g unsalted butter, chilled and cubed
squeeze of lemon juice
2 tbsp chopped fresh chives

PER SERVING
400 cals
25g fat
12g saturated fat
3.5g total sugars
1g salt

PREHEAT THE OVEN TO 200°C/180°FAN/MARK 6. Roll the cod in the flour to coat and season with pepper. Heat the olive oil in a heavy-based frying pan over a high heat until almost smoking. Add the fish, skin-side down, and cook for 2 minutes, then place in a roasting tin, skin-side up, and set aside.

PLACE THE SPINACH IN a large colander and run it under a cold tap to dampen the leaves. Place in a large saucepan and cook over a medium–high heat until just wilted. Remove from the heat, drain, squeezing out all the excess water then season with salt and pepper.

ROAST THE COD IN THE OVEN for 8 minutes or until just opaque and cooked. Leave to rest in a warm place for 5 minutes while you make the sauce.

PLACE THE SHALLOTS IN A SMALL PAN with the wine, vinegar and 3 tablespoons of cold water. Boil until reduced to 1 tablespoon, then stir in the cream and reduce again.

OVER A LOW HEAT, gradually whisk in the butter, piece by piece, until amalgamated; this process shouldn't take too long. Do not allow to boil or become too hot or the sauce will separate; if necessary remove from the heat as you whisk in more butter. Add lemon juice, salt and pepper to taste, and stir in the chives.

REHEAT THE SPINACH, pile onto warmed serving plates, top with a piece of roast cod and pour 3 tablespoons of the sauce over each serving.

79

FISH & SEAFOOD

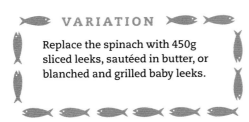

VARIATION

Replace the spinach with 450g sliced leeks, sautéed in butter, or blanched and grilled baby leeks.

Seared Tuna with a Sweet and Sour Marinade

PREPARATION TIME: 10 MINS, *plus marinating* | COOKING TIME: 5 MINS | SERVES 4

In this recipe, the secret of success lies in the tuna being very fresh and the pan being as hot as possible. The high heat seals the outside of the fish and creates a crisp exterior, while the inside remains tender.

450g piece Sainsbury's fresh tuna fillet, about 4–5cm thick
2 tbsp olive oil, plus extra to prepare the tuna
salt and freshly ground black pepper
175g young spinach or rocket leaves, to serve

For the marinade
125ml extra virgin olive oil
juice of 1 lemon
2 tbsp Sainsbury's balsamic vinegar
3 cloves
1 bay leaf
2 tbsp pine nuts
3 tbsp raisins
1 tbsp sugar
¼ tsp dried chilli flakes

PER SERVING
474 cals
33.4g fat
5g saturated fat
13.8g total sugars
0.3g salt

RUB THE TUNA WITH A LITTLE OLIVE OIL and season with salt and pepper. Heat the 2 tablespoons of oil in a heavy-based frying pan or griddle. When it is very hot, add the tuna. Cook over a very high heat for about 1 minute on each side, using two wooden spoons to turn the fish. Make sure it's well browned and verging on crisp on the outside. Alternatively, if you prefer your fish cooked through, cook it over a medium–high heat for 4–5 minutes on each side. Remove from the pan and allow to cool, then wrap in plastic film and refrigerate for 30 minutes.

PREPARE THE MARINADE. In a small bowl mix together the olive oil, lemon juice, balsamic vinegar, cloves, bay leaf, pine nuts, raisins, sugar and chilli flakes.

WHEN THE TUNA IS CHILLED AND FIRM, unwrap and, using a very sharp knife, cut across the grain into thin slices, about 5mm thick. Lay the tuna slices, overlapping, in a shallow glass or earthenware dish and pour over the marinade. Cover and leave to marinate in the fridge for several hours, or overnight if possible.

TAKE THE TUNA OUT OF THE FRIDGE an hour or so before serving to let it come to room temperature. Serve the tuna slices on a bed of spinach or rocket with the marinade spooned over.

VARIATION

Use fresh salmon in place of the tuna.

Stir–fried King Prawns on Sesame Noodles

PREPARATION TIME: 10 MINS | COOKING TIME: 10 MINS | SERVES 4

A fast and sophisticated shellfish dish. It's important that the prawns are raw, but you can buy them in various stages (see TIP). If you serve them with the shells on – which is the prettiest way – it would be a good idea to have finger bowls on the table.

16 By Sainsbury's raw king prawns (see TIP)
2 tsp Sainsbury's sesame seeds
1 tsp salt
150g mangetout, topped and tailed
250g egg noodles
2 tbsp vegetable oil
4 spring onions, trimmed and roughly chopped
8cm piece fresh root ginger, peeled and grated
juice of 1 lime
2 tsp chopped coriander leaves
2 tbsp soy sauce
1 tsp Sainsbury's sesame oil
lime wedges, to serve
prawn crackers, to serve (optional)

PER SERVING
394 cals
13.4g fat
2.5g saturated fat
3.1g total sugars
3.3g salt

IF THE PRAWNS ARE FROZEN, thaw them in advance; if you buy them fresh, keep them refrigerated until you are ready to cook.

PUT THE SESAME SEEDS IN A SMALL, HEAVY-BASED PAN and shake over a medium heat until they begin to turn golden and develop a toasted aroma. Tip the toasted sesame seeds out onto a saucer.

BRING A LARGE PAN OF WATER TO THE BOIL, add the salt and mangetout and return to the boil. Simmer for 30 seconds, then drop in the egg noodles, turn off the heat and leave to stand for 6 minutes.

MEANWHILE, HEAT THE OIL IN A WIDE FRYING PAN. Add the prawns and cook for 1½–2 minutes on each side, scattering over the spring onions and ginger before you turn them. Add the lime juice and sprinkle over the chopped coriander when the prawns are cooked.

DRAIN THE NOODLES AND MANGETOUT and toss them with the soy sauce, sesame oil and toasted sesame seeds. Transfer to a heated serving dish or individual plates and arrange the prawns and spring onions on top. Serve immediately, with the lime wedges and prawn crackers if desired.

TIP

Raw king prawns are available fresh and frozen. Buy fresh ones in their shells and with their heads still on, if possible. They are also sold shelled and headless, and in their shells but with heads removed.

Seared Scallops with Chorizo

PREPARATION TIME: 10 MINS | COOKING TIME: 15 MINS | SERVES 4

A vibrant dish, packed with flavours of the Mediterranean. Finely chopped spicy mini chorizo, shallots and cherry tomatoes combine to make a chunky dressing spooned over melt-in-the-mouth scallops. Take care not to overcook the scallops: sear them for one minute on each side in a hot frying pan so they're still soft in the centre.

100g Sainsbury's mini cooking chorizo, finely chopped
2 shallots, finely chopped
8 cherry tomatoes, quartered
2–3 thyme sprigs
2 tbsp Sainsbury's Spanish sherry vinegar
2 tbsp extra virgin olive oil
1 tbsp olive oil
16 Sainsbury's scallops
salt

PER SERVING
251 cals
15.2g fat
3.9g saturated fat
2g total sugars
0.7g salt

HEAT A SMALL FRYING PAN and add the chorizo – there's no need to add any oil as the chorizo is fatty enough. As soon as the chorizo starts to cook and release its orange oil, add the shallots and cook for 2–3 minutes until golden.

STIR IN THE CHERRY TOMATOES AND THYME and cook until the tomatoes just start to soften. Pour in the vinegar and extra virgin olive oil, season well and take off the heat.

SEASON THE SCALLOPS WITH SALT. Heat the olive oil in a frying pan over a high heat until hot. Add the scallops, four or five at a time and cook for 1 minute on each side. Set aside on a plate and continue until all the scallops are cooked.

DIVIDE THE SCALLOPS BETWEEN FOUR PLATES, spoon over the dressing and serve immediately.

FISH & SEAFOOD

VARIATION

For a main fish course, spoon the chorizo dressing over firm white grilled fish and serve with wilted spinach and new potatoes tossed in butter and parsley.

TIP

You can buy scallops with or without the orange coral or roe. If you buy them with the roe, keep it on and cook it with the scallop or cut it off and fry separately. Like the scallops, the roe needs to be cooked for just 1 minute on each side.

Thai-Style Chilli Squid Curry

PREPARATION TIME: 20 MINS | COOKING TIME: 10–15 MINS | SERVES 4

A popular Mediterranean and Eastern ingredient, squid is the perfect partner to all kinds of spices and its natural richness means it needs little else to make this a simple yet satisfying curry.

440ml half-fat coconut milk
200ml hot fish stock
90g Sainsbury's Thai red curry paste
1 tbsp Thai fish sauce
1 tbsp soy sauce
300g Thai jasmine rice
3 tbsp vegetable or olive oil
4 spring onions, sliced
3 garlic cloves, sliced
2 carrots, thinly sliced
1 red pepper, chopped
1kg raw squid, sliced into rings
6 tbsp fresh lime juice
2 tbsp finely chopped By Sainsbury's coriander leaves
2 tbsp finely chopped basil leaves
1 red chilli, deseeded and finely sliced

PER SERVING
760 cals
28.8g fat
12.2g saturated fat
8.1g total sugars
3.1g salt

PUT THE COCONUT MILK, hot stock, curry paste, fish sauce, and soy sauce into a large pan. Cover and bring to a simmer.

TO COOK THE RICE, pour it into a jug and note the volume, then transfer to a medium pan. Add double the volume of boiling water, cover and bring to a simmer. Turn the heat to its lowest setting and simmer according to the timings on the packet.

HEAT HALF THE OIL IN A FRYING PAN over a high heat and cook the spring onions, garlic, carrots and pepper for 2 minutes until lightly browned. Add to the simmering coconut curry mixture.

HEAT THE REMAINING OIL in the same pan (there's no need to wash it) and fry the squid in the same way.

TRANSFER THE SQUID TO THE CURRY SAUCE to warm through and add the lime juice, coriander, basil and chilli. Serve immediately with the rice.

TIP

Squid has a tender texture but needs to be cooked either quickly, as in this recipe, or braised slowly, otherwise it can become rubbery.

Seafood Risotto

PREPARATION TIME: 15 MINS | COOKING TIME: 45 MINS | SERVES 6

Slow cooking and patience at the hob are key to making a good risotto. By adding the stock slowly and steadily, and stirring it in continuously, the rice softens gradually in the hot liquid until cooked. Stir in a generous knob of butter and grated Parmesan at the end to bring together all the ingredients and transform them into a rich, creamy pot of rice.

3 tbsp olive oil
1 onion, chopped
3 garlic cloves, chopped
1.5 litres hot fish stock
500g Sainsbury's Arborio risotto rice
1 bay leaf
1 tsp paprika
250ml white wine
100g Sainsbury's grated Parmesan
50g butter, diced
500g mixed seafood, such as raw sliced squid, prawns and scallops
12 cherry tomatoes, halved
salt and freshly ground black pepper

PER SERVING
650 cals
18.8g fat
8.6g saturated fat
1.9g total sugars
1.5g salt

HEAT 2 TABLESPOONS OF OIL in a large pan over a medium heat and cook the onion and garlic for about 10 minutes until soft but not coloured. Pour the stock into a separate pan and heat gently.

STIR THE RICE, BAY LEAF AND PAPRIKA into the onion mixture and cook for 1–2 minutes to heat up the rice. Pour in the wine and bring the mixture to the boil, allowing it to simmer and reduce and cook off the alcohol.

LADLE THE STOCK INTO THE PAN OF RICE, a ladleful at a time, allowing each to be absorbed into the rice before adding another. Stir continuously as the stock is added. Once all the stock has been added, season well with salt and pepper and stir in half the Parmesan and the butter. Keep on a very low simmer.

HEAT THE REMAINING TABLESPOON OF OIL in a large frying pan over a medium heat and add the seafood. Cook for 3–5 minutes, tossing everything around in the pan until cooked. The scallops should be golden, but meltingly soft inside. The prawns will have turned pink and opaque and the squid will have turned from a translucent colour to being slightly curled up and golden. Add the cherry tomatoes and cook for a further 1–2 minutes. Season well.

DIVIDE THE RISOTTO BETWEEN SIX WARMED PLATES and spoon the seafood on top. Serve with the remaining Parmesan and freshly ground black pepper.

89

FISH & SEAFOOD

TIP

If you want to prepare the risotto ahead, cook it until half the stock has been absorbed. Spread out on a tray to cool the mixture quickly then transfer to a sealed container and chill for up to 6 hours. To finish cooking, put the par-cooked risotto in a pan and heat gently. Bring the remaining stock to a simmer in a separate pan, then gradually start to add it and complete the recipe, as above.

Steamed Mussels with White Wine Sauce

PREPARATION TIME: 20 MINS | COOKING TIME: 10 MINS | SERVES 4

This classic French dish, *moules marinières*, is quick to cook and simply needs some crusty bread to mop up the garlicky juices. Make sure the mussels are alive before cooking them by tapping the shell and checking they close.

1kg By Sainsbury's Chilean mussels
knob of butter
1 tsp olive oil
2 shallots, finely chopped
1 garlic clove, chopped
200ml dry white wine
2–3 tbsp freshly chopped By Sainsbury's parsley
salt and freshly ground black pepper
crusty bread, to serve

PER SERVING
133 cals
4.6g fat
1.7g saturated fat
1g total sugars
0.6g salt

PUT THE MUSSELS IN A BOWL OF COLD WATER and scrub each well, removing any beards (see page 31). Discard any that are cracked, broken or remain open when tapped. Drain the mussels in a colander and give them a good rinse.

PUT THE BUTTER AND OIL IN A LARGE PAN and place over a medium heat. When the butter has stopped foaming, add the shallots and cook for 2–3 minutes to soften. Stir in the garlic and cook for 1 minute. Season well.

POUR IN THE WHITE WINE and bring to the boil. Simmer to reduce by half and cook off the alcohol. Tip in the drained mussels, then cover with a lid immediately to trap any steam. Cook for 6–8 minutes until all the mussels have opened (discard any that remain closed. Give the pan a good shake half way through cooking.

WHEN ALL THE MUSSELS HAVE OPENED, sprinkle with parsley, toss again and spoon into bowls to serve with the bread.

VARIATION

For a cream sauce, cook 1 finely chopped celery stalk with the shallots. After cooking the mussels, pour in 150ml double cream. Put the lid on again and give the pan a good shake to warm the cream through and toss all the mussels in the sauce. Taste for seasoning, then serve.

Poultry & Meat

Tandoori Chicken with Minted Couscous

PREPARATION TIME: 20 MINS, *plus marinating* | COOKING TIME: 10–15 MINS | SERVES 4

Marinating bite-sized pieces of chicken in a spicy yoghurt dressing leaves it beautifully tender. The dressing for the couscous is sweet but balances the tangy flavours of the chicken perfectly.

300ml Sainsbury's Greek-style yoghurt
2 garlic cloves, crushed
2.5cm piece of fresh root ginger, peeled and grated
finely grated zest and juice of ½ lemon
2 tsp hot curry paste
1 tsp paprika
½ tsp salt
750g By Sainsbury's skinless chicken breast, cut into 2.5cm cubes
225g quick-cook couscous
225ml Sainsbury's Signature hot chicken or vegetable stock
4 ripe tomatoes, skinned, deseeded and diced
1 small red onion, finely chopped
25g mint leaves, chopped, plus extra to garnish
50g sultanas
125g cucumber, peeled, halved lengthways and finely sliced
lemon wedges, to garnish

For the dressing
juice of 2 lemons
25g caster sugar
4 tbsp extra virgin olive oil
salt and freshly ground black pepper

PUT THE YOGHURT IN A LARGE BOWL with the garlic, ginger, lemon zest and juice, curry paste, paprika and salt. Add the chicken pieces, toss well to coat and leave to marinate in the fridge for up to 8 hours.

WHEN READY TO COOK THE CHICKEN, put the couscous in a large bowl. Pour over the hot stock, then cover and set aside for 20 minutes. Once all the liquid has been absorbed, take a fork and pull it through the couscous to fluff up the grains.

TO MAKE THE DRESSING, put the lemon juice and sugar in a pan and heat gently until dissolved. Stir in the olive oil and season to taste, then remove from the heat.

TRANSFER THE COUSCOUS TO A LARGE BOWL, add half the dressing and stir with a fork until evenly mixed. Stir in the tomatoes, onion, mint and sultanas, season to taste and set aside. Toss the cucumber in a bowl with the remaining dressing and set aside.

PREHEAT THE GRILL TO HIGH. Remove the chicken from the marinade and thread onto 8 skewers. Grill for 10–15 minutes, turning frequently, until the chicken is charred on the outside and cooked right through (push a sharp knife into a cube to check there are no pink juices). Leave to cool.

SPOON THE COUSCOUS ONTO INDIVIDUAL PLATES and top with the skewers. Serve with the cucumber salad and garnish with lemon wedges and mint.

94

POULTRY & MEAT

PER SERVING
583 cals
18.8g fat
5.3g saturated fat
19.9g total sugars
1.3g salt

VARIATION
Replace the chicken fillet with skinless monkfish fillet. Cube, marinate and cook as above for 10–12 minutes until the fish is opaque.

TIP
If using bamboo skewers, pre-soak them in cold water for 30 minutes and cover with foil when grilling to prevent them scorching under the heat.

Chicken Pie

PREPARATION TIME: 20 MINS | COOKING TIME: 30 MINS | SERVES 8

This is equally good made with chicken or turkey, and is ideal for using up Christmas leftovers. If possible, use a piece of home-cooked gammon or ham cut into generous chunks. Alternatively, buy a thick slice of good-quality ham so you can cut it into bite-sized pieces by hand. You could also use chunks of salami.

2 leeks, trimmed and cut into 2cm slices
350g Sainsbury's Be Good To Yourself soft cheese
1 egg
1 tsp mustard
3 tbsp chopped fresh parsley
1 tsp finely grated lemon zest
700g By Sainsbury's cooked chicken or turkey, cut into bite-sized pieces
about 175g cooked gammon or ham, cut into bite-sized pieces
500g pack By Sainsbury's ready-made puff pastry
1 egg, beaten, to glaze
salt and freshly ground black pepper

PER SERVING
470 cals
23.3g fat
10g saturated fat
2.7g total sugars
1.5g salt

PREHEAT THE OVEN TO 200°C/180°FAN/MARK 6. Bring a small pan of water to the boil. Add the leeks, bring to the boil again and cook for about 2 minutes or until slightly softened. Drain thoroughly, reserving three tablespoons of the cooking liquid.

PUT THE SOFT CHEESE IN A BOWL and mix with the reserved cooking liquid. Gradually beat in the egg, then add the mustard, parsley, lemon zest and plenty of salt and pepper. Fold in the chicken or turkey, with the gammon or ham and the leeks. Place a pie funnel into the middle of a 1.2–1.4 litre round pie dish, then spoon the mixture around it.

ROLL OUT THE PASTRY on a lightly floured surface and trim to a round about 5cm larger than the pie dish. Cut off a 2.5cm strip from all round the edge and press it onto the rim of the pie dish.

BRUSH THE PASTRY RIM WITH A LITTLE BEATEN EGG. Position the pastry round on top to make a lid. Cut a hole where the pie funnel is resting and gently push the pastry down over it. Use a finger or thumb to seal the two layers of pastry together, then using a sharp knife, knock up the edges. Do this by tapping the blade against the outer edge of the pastry to create lines. This helps to ensure the layers of the pastry rise.

DECORATE WITH LEAVES CUT FROM THE PASTRY TRIMMINGS. Brush the pastry thoroughly with beaten egg.

STAND THE PIE ON A BAKING SHEET. Bake in the oven for about 30 minutes or until the pastry is well risen and golden brown. Leave to rest for 15 minutes before cutting and serving.

VARIATION
Omit the mustard and flavour the sauce instead with 25–50g crumbled Stilton.

Roast Chicken with Stuffing Balls and a Rich Gravy

PREPARATION TIME: 30 MINS | COOKING TIME: 1½ HOURS | SERVES 4–6

Seasoning a chicken both inside and out is key to ensuring it has a really good flavour. Roasting the joint of meat over a bed of chopped vegetables and water produces a ready-made base for the gravy.

1 onion, sliced
1 carrot, roughly
    chopped
1 celery stick, roughly
    chopped
a few sprigs of thyme
2–3 whole garlic cloves
1 Sainsbury's Taste The
    Difference free range
    chicken, about 1.75kg
½ lemon
1 tbsp plain flour
300ml hot Sainsbury's
    Signature chicken
    stock
300100ml white wine
1 tbsp redcurrant jelly
salt and freshly ground
    black pepper

For the stuffing balls
4 pork sausages
75g breadcrumbs
1 egg, beaten
1 shallot, finely chopped
1 tbsp chopped parsley
1 tbsp chopped thyme
    leaves
olive oil

PER SERVING
400 cals
11g fat
3.5g saturated fat
4.8g total sugars
1.4g salt

PREHEAT THE OVEN TO 200°C/180°FAN/MARK 6. Put the chopped vegetables, thyme and garlic into a roasting tin. Place the chicken on top, push the lemon into the cavity and season well inside and all over. Pour 300ml boiling water into the tin and roast in the oven for 20 minutes per 450g plus 20 minutes. To check the chicken is cooked, pierce the thigh with a skewer and push the skin to see whether the juices run clear. If there are any pink juices, return to the oven and cook for a further 5–10 minutes.

MEANWHILE, PREPARE THE STUFFING BALLS. Squeeze the sausage meat out of its casing into a bowl. Stir in 50g of the breadcrumbs, the egg, shallot and herbs and season well.

PUT THE REMAINING BREADCRUMBS into a shallow bowl. Wet your hands and shape the sausage mixture into 12 small balls. Toss each ball in breadcrumbs and put in a shallow ovenproof tin or dish. Drizzle with oil. Put in the oven 10 minutes before the end of the chicken's cooking time and cook for 20 minutes.

TAKE THE CHICKEN OUT OF THE OVEN and put on a warm plate. Cover and set aside to rest.

MEANWHILE, MAKE THE GRAVY. Drain the fat from the tin, leaving behind the meat juices and about 1 tablespoon of the fat. Stir in the flour, place over a medium heat and cook for 1–2 minutes until bubbling. Gradually stir in the stock, wine and jelly and bring to the boil. Simmer for 2–3 minutes. Strain through a sieve into a jug. Push the vegetables with a wooden spoon to extract all the juices for maximum flavour. Check the seasoning in the gravy then serve with the chicken.

99

POULTRY & MEAT

TIP
You can eat the vegetables left in the sieve as well – they're delicious spread on bread with a little leftover chicken.

Spatchcock Chicken with Garlic and Rosemary

PREPARATION TIME: 15 MINS, *plus marinating* | **COOKING TIME: 40 MINS** | **SERVES 4**

Learning how to spatchcock a chicken is a great skill. Not only does it cook in half the time of a roast chicken, but it can also be flavoured with whatever herbs and spices you have to hand. Roast in the oven, or over the coals of a barbecue, to infuse it with delicious smoky flavours.

1 whole By Sainsbury's chicken, about 1.5kg
½ teaspoon each salt and freshly ground black pepper
2 garlic cloves, crushed
2 tbsp olive oil
leaves from 1 bushy rosemary sprig, chopped
1 lemon, cut into wedges

PER SERVING
335 cals
10.7g fat
2.2g saturated fat
0.8g total sugars
0.88g salt

PUT THE CHICKEN ON A BOARD and turn it upside down so it is resting on its breast. Take a sharp pair of scissors and cut along one side of the backbone. Do the same with the other side to remove the backbone completely.

TURN THE CHICKEN OVER AND PRESS, with the heel of your hand, in the middle of the breastbone – you should hear it crack – to flatten it. Push a wooden or metal skewer diagonally through the leg of one side of the chicken and through the breast on the other side. Then do the same on the opposite side.

WORK THE SALT AND PEPPER INTO THE CRUSHED GARLIC, then stir in the olive oil and rosemary. Brush the mixture all over the skin of the chicken. Put in a sealable container and marinate in the fridge for at least 30 minutes and up to 6 hours.

PREHEAT THE OVEN TO 200°C/180°FAN/MARK 6. Put the chicken in a roasting tin with the lemon wedges and roast for 40 minutes. To check the chicken is cooked, pierce the thickest part of the leg with a sharp knife and press the flesh – the juices should run clear. If they're still pink, return to the oven and test again after 5–10 minutes.

LET THE COOKED CHICKEN REST for 10 minutes before carving. Cut off the legs and halve each into drumstick and thigh, then carve each breast in half. Serve with the lemon wedges.

TIP
Make sure you wash your hands well after spatchcocking the chicken to avoid contaminating other ingredients and kitchen surfaces.

Moroccan Turkey and Butterbean Stew with Couscous

PREPARATION TIME: 20 MINS | COOKING TIME: 25–30 MINS | SERVES 4

The real flavour boost in this recipe comes from the harissa. This Middle Eastern paste, made with red pepper, chilli and spices, is combined with chunks of turkey and vegetables in a heavenly stew and served with a simple couscous salad. Couscous is easy to prepare: use the same volume of stock to weight of couscous.

500g By Sainsbury's turkey breast, chopped into bite-sized pieces
1 tbsp By Sainsbury's harissa spices
1 tsp ground ginger
1 tsp ground cumin
½ tsp ground coriander
½ tsp ground cinnamon
2 tbsp olive oil
1 onion, roughly chopped
1 aubergine, roughly chopped
1 garlic clove, crushed
1 red pepper, roughly chopped
½ butternut squash, peeled and roughly chopped
400g can butterbeans, drained
400g can chopped tomatoes
300ml hot chicken stock
8 green olives
salt and freshly ground black pepper

For the couscous
300g couscous
300ml hot chicken stock
1 tbsp olive oil
grated zest and juice of 1 lemon
2 tbsp chopped parsley, plus extra to garnish.

PER SERVING
546 cals
12.2g fat
1.9g saturated fat
11.8g total sugars
1.5g salt

PUT THE TURKEY IN A BOWL and add half of the harissa and half the spices. Mix well and set aside.

HEAT THE OIL IN A LARGE PAN and fry the onion and aubergine for 5–10 minutes until softened and golden. Stir in the remaining harissa and spices along with the garlic, red pepper and squash and cook for 2–3 minutes.

SCOOP THE VEGETABLES ONTO A PLATE and add the turkey to the pan. Fry quickly until browned, then return the vegetables to the pan with the butterbeans, tomatoes, stock and olives. Season well with salt and pepper, cover and bring to the boil. Simmer for 20 minutes until the stew has thickened.

MEANWHILE, POUR THE COUSCOUS INTO A BOWL and pour over the stock. Cover and leave to soak for 20 minutes. Fluff up with a fork, then stir in the oil, lemon zest and juice and parsley. Divide between four plates, spoon the stew on top and garnish with parsley.

102

TIP

Canned butterbeans are easy to use, but if you have more time, and want to save money too, use dried. Soak 125g dried beans in a bowl of cold water overnight. When ready to cook, drain well and put in a pan. Cover with cold water again and add a bay leaf, ¼ onion, 1 roughly chopped carrot and 1 stick of celery. Bring to the boil and simmer for 1–1½ hours until the beans are tender. Follow the recipe, using the stock that the beans are cooked in for the stew.

Pan-Fried Duck with a Sour-Cherry and Five-spice Sauce

PREPARATION TIME: 15 MINS, *plus marinating* | **COOKING TIME: 30 MINS** | **SERVES 4**

The skin on duck is very fatty so it needs to be cooked skin-side down in a hot pan first to render down the fat. Rest the meat after cooking to allow the juices to run through it, leaving the meat deliciously tender, then add the juices to the sauce. Serve with rice and steamed asparagus and Chantenay carrots.

25g Sainsbury's sour cherries
4 By Sainsbury's duck breasts
1 tbsp olive oil
2 tsp Chinese five-spice powder
300ml hot Sainsbury's Signature chicken stock
75ml red wine
4 star anise
1 tbsp redcurrant jelly
salt and freshly ground black pepper

PER SERVING
323 cals
14.2g fat
3.9g saturated fat
6.5g total sugars
0.7g salt

PUT THE SOUR CHERRIES IN A SMALL BOWL and pour over enough boiling water to cover. Put the duck breasts on a board and use a sharp knife to slice diagonally through the fatty skin on top of each piece three or four times.

MIX TOGETHER THE OIL AND FIVE-SPICE and brush all over the duck. Transfer to a sealable container and leave to marinate for at least 30 minutes and up to 4 hours.

PREHEAT THE OVEN TO 200°C/180°FAN/MARK 6. Heat a large frying pan and fry the duck, skin-side down, two pieces at a time, until dark golden.

TURN THE DUCK OVER and briefly cook the other side. Put in a flameproof roasting tin then repeat with the other two duck breasts. Roast for 15 minutes. (See TIP below for how to reuse the fat in the pan.)

TAKE THE DUCK BREASTS OUT OF THE ROASTING TIN, put on a warm plate, cover with foil and leave to rest. Carefully drain away all the fat in the tin, leaving behind just the meat juices. (The fat floats on top, so will be easy to separate.) Put the roasting tin on the hob and add the stock, wine, star anise and redcurrant jelly. Season with salt and pepper. Bring to the boil and simmer for 3–4 minutes until syrupy. Stir in the sour cherries and their soaking water and any juices from the rested meat and heat through. Slice the duck and serve with the sauce drizzled over.

TIP

Save any fat that comes out of the duck and transfer to a clean, sterilised jar. Store in the fridge and use within 2 weeks to make crispy roast potatoes.

Garlic and Honey Pork with Vegetable Noodle Broth

PREPARATION TIME: 20 MINS, *plus marinating* | **COOKING TIME: 25 MINS** | **SERVES 4**

Pork tenderloin is a cut that cooks very quickly (see pages 38–9 for more information on the different cuts of pork). Pan-fry it first to seal in all the flavour of the marinade, then finish off by roasting it in the oven. Slice and serve on top of a clear noodle soup packed full of vegetables.

500g Sainsbury's pork tenderloin
3 garlic cloves, crushed
5cm piece of fresh root ginger, peeled and grated
2 tbsp By Sainsbury's clear honey
1 tbsp soy sauce
3 tbsp dry sherry
1 tbsp vegetable oil, plus extra for frying

For the vegetable noodle broth
grated zest and juice of ½ lemon
1 tbsp sesame oil
2 tbsp vegetable oil
1 large yellow pepper, cored, deseeded and finely sliced
4 spring onions, trimmed and sliced diagonally
2 By Sainsbury's lemongrass stalks, coarse outer stalks removed then shredded finely
2 tsp sesame seeds
800ml hot Sainsbury's Signature chicken stock
125g By Sainsbury's rice noodles
225g beansprouts, rinsed and drained

PER SERVING
527 cals
20.7g fat
4.1g saturated fat
11.8g total sugars
1.4g salt

PREHEAT THE OVEN TO 220°C/200°FAN/MARK 7. Trim any fat and membrane from the pork tenderloins and prick them all over with a fork. Mix the garlic, ginger, honey, soy sauce, sherry and oil together in a shallow non-metallic dish, then add the pork tenderloins and coat all over in the mixture. Set aside to marinate for 20 minutes or, if preparing ahead, cover and chill for up to 8 hours.

HEAT A LITTLE OIL IN A FRYING PAN and brown the pork all over. Transfer to a roasting tin and roast for 15–20 minutes, turning the pork and basting with the juices halfway through the cooking time. When the meat is cooked, switch the oven off, leaving the meat inside.

MEANWHILE, PREPARE THE BROTH. Mix the lemon zest and juice with the sesame oil. Heat the vegetable oil in a wok or sauté pan, add the pepper, spring onions (reserving a few for garnish), lemongrass and sesame seeds and stir-fry for 1 minute. Pour in the stock, and the lemon zest and juice mixture, then add the noodles. Cover, bring to the boil then simmer following the timings on the noodle packet. Stir in the beansprouts.

TRANSFER THE PORK TENDERLOIN to a carving board. Pour the liquid from the roasting tin into the broth. Carve the meat into slices about 5mm thick. Ladle the broth into four bowls, top with the sliced pork and garnish with the reserved spring onions.

VARIATION

This recipe is delicious with prawns, too. Use 500g shelled raw king prawns and marinate as for pork. Stir-fry the prawns in a wok or sauté pan over a medium heat with a drizzle of oil until pink, then spoon on top of the broth.

Gammon with Boston Baked Beans

PREPARATION TIME: 20 MINS | COOKING TIME: 1¾ HOURS | SERVES 6 | ✳

This recipe is a real crowd-pleaser and will easily serve more if teamed with a baked potato, crusty bread and a crisp salad on the side. A gammon joint is a cheap cut of meat and is rich in flavour so a little goes a long way. If you want to save time, buy a ready-roasted gammon shank and simmer the bean stew on its own for half the time.

1 tbsp sunflower oil
2 onions, roughly chopped
2 carrots, roughly chopped
5 garlic cloves, roughly chopped
400g Sainsbury's gammon joint
2 x 400g cans chopped tomatoes
2 x 400g cans Sainsbury's cannellini beans in water, drained and rinsed
2 x 400g cans Sainsbury's kidney beans in water, drained and rinsed
2 x 400g cans Sainsbury's butterbeans in water, drained and rinsed
2 tbsp Dijon mustard
2 tbsp tomato purée
450ml hot chicken or vegetable stock
1 tsp paprika
50g dark muscovado sugar
3 tbsp black treacle
2 tsp ground cinnamon
2 tbsp Worcestershire sauce
salt and freshly ground black pepper

HEAT THE OIL OVER A MEDIUM HEAT in a large, lidded flameproof casserole and cook the onions, carrots and garlic for about 10 minutes until softened.

ADD ALL THE REMAINING INGREDIENTS, season with salt and pepper, then cover with a lid and bring to a gentle boil. Reduce the heat to a low simmer and cook for 1½ hours until the joint is tender (slice a small piece off the edge to check).

AT THE END OF THE COOKING TIME, remove the ham from the stew and carve the meat off the bone. Serve the sliced ham with the beans.

TIP

This recipe can be frozen for up to 1 month. Once the ham is cooked, lift it out of the bean stew and cool both. Freeze the stew in a sealable container, then wrap the ham well in plastic film and freeze.

PER SERVING
538 cals
12g fat
3.3g saturated fat
24.9g total sugars
2.9g salt

Sausage, Red Onion and Bean Casserole

PREPARATION TIME: 20 MINS | COOKING TIME: 45–55 MINS | SERVES 6 | ❄

This is great for a midweek family supper. Chilli flakes give a fiery heat to the finished dish and are a very handy way of adding spice. There's no need to scrub your hands and the chopping board as you would after preparing a fresh chilli. Plus the level of heat is consistent (unlike fresh chillies where the heat levels vary between each one), so you can add as little or as much as you prefer.

2 tbsp sunflower oil
2 red onions, diced
1 carrot, diced
2 garlic cloves, chopped
½ tsp By Sainsbury's chilli flakes
200ml hot Sainsbury's Signature beef stock
2 x 400g cans chopped tomatoes
420g can pinto beans in water, drained and rinsed
1 tbsp chopped rosemary
450g spicy beef sausages
450g Sainsbury's Taste The Difference Ultimate outdoor bred pork sausages
50g baby leaf spinach
salt and freshly ground black pepper

HEAT 2 TABLESPOONS OF OIL OVER A MEDIUM HEAT in a large flameproof casserole and add the onions and carrot. Cook for 5 minutes until the vegetables are starting to turn golden and caramelise.

STIR IN THE GARLIC AND CHILLI FLAKES and cook for about 1 minute. Pour in the stock, tomatoes, beans and rosemary. Cover and bring to a gentle simmer.

MEANWHILE, HEAT THE REMAINING OIL over a medium heat in a frying pan and cook the sausages for about 10 minutes until browned all over (see TIP below).

ADD THE SAUSAGES TO THE BEANS and continue to simmer, covered, for about 30–40 minutes, checking the level of the liquid regularly. If it looks as if it's becoming too dry, stir in 150ml boiling water.

JUST BEFORE THE END OF THE COOKING TIME, season the casserole well with salt and pepper, stir in the spinach and allow to wilt, then serve.

POULTRY & MEAT

PER SERVING
488 cals
32g fat
10.9g saturated fat
10.2g total sugars
3.5g salt

TIP

As sausages are very fatty, it's best to cook them in a separate pan. That way, once they are browned, you can drain away any fat before adding them to the stew.

VARIATION

For a no-fuss version of cassoulet, the rich slow-cooked casserole from the South of France, fry a couple of rashers of bacon with the onions and carrots at the start of cooking. Leave out the chilli and use pork sausages and haricot beans in place of the beef sausages and the pinto beans. Omit the spinach and 10 minutes before the end of cooking, sprinkle with breadcrumbs. Grill until golden.

Gammon Steaks with a Cucumber, Mango and Chilli Salsa

PREPARATION TIME: 15 MINS | COOKING TIME: 5 MINS | SERVES 4

Gammon steaks make the ideal midweek supper as they're very quick to cook: grill them and they're ready in 5 minutes. Here they are teamed with a chilli-spiced mango salsa whose sweetness is a good match for the salty taste of the gammon. To check a mango is ripe, squeeze it gently to feel it yielding slightly under pressure or sniff the skin: it should smell fragrant. Serve the gammon with a handful of rocket for an easy accompaniment.

1 mango, peeled, stoned and diced
¼ cucumber, quartered, deseeded and diced
10 cherry tomatoes, roughly chopped
1 By Sainsbury's fresh green chilli, deseeded and diced
2 tbsp olive oil, plus extra for brushing
grated zest and juice of 1 lime, plus lime wedges, to serve
½ tsp sugar
1 tbsp chopped fresh coriander
1 tbsp chopped chives
4 x 175g Sainsbury's unsmoked gammon steaks
salt and freshly ground black pepper

PER SERVING
374 cals
19.5g fat
6.1g saturated fat
6.8g total sugars
6.5g salt

PUT THE MANGO, cucumber, cherry tomatoes and chilli in a bowl. Whisk together the oil, lime zest and juice and sugar and pour over the salsa. Season well with salt and pepper, then stir in the herbs.

PREHEAT THE GRILL TO HIGH. Brush a little of the oil over the gammon steaks and season both sides. Grill the gammon for about 2–3 minutes on each side.

DIVIDE THE STEAKS BETWEEN FOUR PLATES, spoon over the salsa and serve each with a wedge of lime.

TIP
To ripen mangoes, put them in a brown paper bag and leave at room temperature for a day or two.

Pork Casserole with Mustard Dumplings

PREPARATION TIME: 20 MINS | COOKING TIME: 1–1½ HOURS | SERVES 6

Pork shoulder is a cheap cut, but needs long, slow cooking to ensure it is really tender. This recipe is a great alternative to a Sunday roast, and simply needs some crusty bread on the side to mop up the juices.

1kg Sainsbury's pork shoulder, cut into 2.5cm cubes
2 tbsp sunflower oil
1 leek, trimmed and roughly chopped
1 onion, roughly chopped
1 turnip, roughly chopped
1 carrot, roughly chopped
1 celery stick, roughly chopped
200g Sainsbury's smoked streaky bacon, each rasher cut into 3
1 thyme sprig
1 bay leaf
200g dried prunes, stoned
100ml beer
300ml hot Sainsbury's Signature chicken stock
½ Savoy cabbage, shredded
salt and freshly ground black pepper

For the dumplings
75g vegetable suet
75g self-raising flour
2 tsp mustard powder
1–2 tbsp freshly chopped parsley

PER SERVING
580 cals
30.4g fat
11.3g saturated fat
16.6g total sugars
1.7g salt

PREHEAT THE OVEN TO 180°C/160°FAN/MARK 4. Season the pork with salt and pepper. Heat 1 tablespoon of oil in a large pan over a high heat and cook the pork until browned all over. Remove with a slotted spoon and set aside.

HEAT THE REMAINING OIL IN THE PAN over a medium heat and cook the leek, onion, turnip, carrot, celery and bacon for about 10 minutes until softened. Stir in the thyme and bay leaf, then place the pork back in the pan.

ADD THE PRUNES, BEER AND STOCK, mix well and season with salt and pepper. Transfer to the oven and cook for 1–1½ hours until the pork is tender.

START MAKING THE DUMPLINGS about 30 minutes before the end of the cooking time. Mix together the suet, flour and mustard powder in a bowl, add seasoning and set aside.

ABOUT 20 MINUTES BEFORE THE END of the cooking time, stir the cabbage into the casserole.

STIR 60ML WATER QUICKLY INTO THE SUET MIX until it forms a dough. Divide roughly into six and spoon each portion on top of the casserole. Cover and cook for 15 minutes.

TO SERVE, DIVIDE THE STEW INTO BOWLS, top each portion with a dumpling and pour over a good amount of sauce.

115

POULTRY & MEAT

TIP
It's important not to overmix the dumplings – just a light touch is required – otherwise they'll taste heavy and stodgy when cooked. In place of the mustard powder, you could stir in 2 teaspoons of Dijon or wholegrain mustard.

Lamb Biryani

PREPARATION TIME: 30 MINS, *plus 30 minutes soaking* | **COOKING TIME: 1 HOUR** | **SERVES 6**

This classic Indian one-pot dish is a celebratory feast combining rich spices, tender lamb and fine-textured basmati rice. It's important to fry the onions over a medium heat in order to brown them quickly – this gives the finished dish a good depth of flavour. Serve with a side of yoghurt mixed with a pinch of chilli powder.

6 tbsp vegetable or sunflower oil

1kg British boneless lamb shoulder, cut into 1.5cm pieces

2 onions, chopped

3 garlic cloves, chopped

5cm piece of fresh root ginger, peeled and chopped

1 bay leaf

2 tsp coriander seeds, crushed

2 tsp cumin seeds

1 tsp chilli flakes

200g brown basmati rice, soaked in cold water for 30 minutes, then washed

2 tbsp tomato purée

100ml coconut milk

100ml natural yoghurt

600ml hot lamb stock

25g By Sainsbury's mint, chopped

25g fresh coriander, chopped

6 spring onions, finely sliced

salt and freshly ground black pepper

By Sainsbury's mango chutney, to serve

HEAT HALF THE OIL IN A LARGE PAN over a high heat and brown the lamb. Season well with salt and pepper then remove with a slotted spoon and set aside.

HEAT THE REMAINING OIL in the pan over a medium heat and fry the onions, garlic, ginger, bay leaf, coriander and cumin seeds and chilli flakes for 2 minutes until the spices are aromatic and the onion is softened and turning golden. Mix in the rice and browned lamb then stir in the tomato purée.

POUR OVER THE COCONUT MILK, yoghurt and stock and stir all the ingredients together. Cover and cook on the lowest heat setting at a very gentle bubble for 1 hour until all the liquid has been absorbed and the lamb is tender.

JUST BEFORE SERVING, combine the mint, coriander and spring onions and sprinkle the mix over the biryani. Serve with the mango chutney on the side.

VARIATION

For a vegetarian version, omit the lamb and use vegetable stock instead. Serve with hard-boiled quartered eggs sprinkled with a little chilli powder.

TIP

Freeze any leftover coconut milk in a sealable container for up to 1 month.

PER SERVING
558 cals
27.9g fat
10.2g saturated fat
4.5g total sugars
0.6g salt

Lamb Cutlets with Mint, Caper and Anchovy Dressing

PREPARATION TIME: 15 MINS | COOKING TIME: 15 MINS | SERVES 4

Lamb cutlets are the chops cut and prepared from a rack of lamb (see pages 37–8 for more information on the different cuts of lamb). Trimmed, the eye of the cutlet is rich in flavour. This recipe, using anchovies, lemon and capers, provides an alternative twist to the traditional combination of lamb and mint. Serve with new potatoes and steamed carrots for an easy, yet impressive, main course.

8 Sainsbury's British lamb cutlets, trimmed
2 tbsp olive oil
25g butter
1 shallot, finely chopped
4 Sainsbury's anchovy fillets, finely chopped
grated zest and juice of 1 lemon
1 tbsp capers
1 tbsp chopped mint
salt and freshly ground black pepper

PER SERVING
411 cals
27g fat
11g saturated fat
0.4g total sugars
0.97g salt

PREHEAT THE OVEN TO 110°C/90°FAN/MARK ¼. Brush the cutlets with oil and season all over with salt and pepper. Heat a large frying pan until hot and brown the cutlets on each side, in batches, until golden on the outside but still pink in the middle. Put in a roasting tin, cover with foil and keep warm in the oven.

PUT THE BUTTER AND ANY REMAINING OIL IN A PAN and heat gently. When the butter stops foaming, add the shallot and cook for 2–3 minutes until golden. Take the pan off the heat and stir in the anchovies, lemon zest and juice, capers and mint. Season with pepper – there's no need for any salt as the anchovies are salty. Spoon over the lamb and serve.

VARIATION

This sauce would work equally well with chicken breasts. Pan-fry the chicken breasts until golden, then transfer to a roasting tin and roast in the oven, preheated to 200°C/180°Fan/Mark 6, for 20–25 minutes. Check the juices run clear by piercing the thickest part with a sharp knife.

119

POULTRY & MEAT

Lamb Shanks with Redcurrant and Rosemary

PREPARATION TIME: 30 MINS | COOKING TIME: 1½–2 HOURS | SERVES 6 | ❄

Here's a wholesome serving of meat, vegetables and a rich sauce. The stew can be left in a low oven to simmer away, leaving the lamb melt-in-the-mouth tender. Serve simply with a green vegetable, such as green beans, to cut through the richness.

6 Sainsbury's British lamb shanks, dusted with a little plain flour
3 tbsp sunflower oil
200ml red wine
1 leek, chopped
2 onions, cut into wedges
6 small turnips, quartered
250g Sainsbury's British Chantenay carrots, trimmed
700g small new potatoes
6 rosemary sprigs, finely chopped
3 bay leaves
1.3 litres hot Sainsbury's Signature beef stock
1 tbsp Dijon mustard
5 tbsp By Sainsbury's redcurrant jelly
1 tbsp red wine vinegar
3 tbsp chopped parsley
salt and freshly ground black pepper

PREHEAT THE OVEN TO 160°C/140°FAN/MARK 3. Season the lamb shanks with salt and pepper. Heat 2 tablespoons of the oil in a large frying pan over a high heat and cook the lamb for about 10 minutes until browned all over. Transfer to a large ovenproof, lidded casserole.

WHILE THE FRYING PAN IS STILL HOT, add the red wine, bring to the boil, then simmer for a few minutes to cook off the alcohol. Pour over the lamb.

HEAT THE REMAINING OIL in the frying pan over a medium heat, then add the leek, onions, turnips, carrots and potatoes and cook for 10 minutes. Add the vegetables to the casserole, along with the rosemary, bay leaves, stock, mustard, redcurrant jelly and vinegar. Add seasoning and cook in the oven for 1½–2 hours, checking and turning the shanks halfway through the cooking time.

ABOUT 5 MINUTES BEFORE THE END of the cooking time, add the chopped parsley.

PER SERVING
594 cals
22.6g fat
7.8g saturated fat
18.6g total sugars
1.2g salt

VARIATION

Omit the potatoes from the recipe and serve the lamb with mashed potato (see page 126) on the side instead.

Lamb Meatballs with Dill Sauce

PREPARATION TIME: 30 MINS | COOKING TIME: 1¼ HOURS | SERVES 6 | ❄

Cinnamon adds a hint of spice to these delicate fine-textured meatballs, which are served with a creamy wine and dill-flavoured sauce. If you can't get hold of fresh dill, substitute it with dried. You will need only one or two teaspoons, however, as it has a more concentrated flavour.

600g Sainsbury's British minced lamb
6 spring onions, trimmed
175g Sainsbury's unsmoked back bacon, roughly chopped
1 garlic clove
pinch of ground cinnamon
3 tbsp olive oil
450ml dry white wine
600g Sainsbury's tagliatelle pasta, to serve
15g butter
4 tbsp chopped fresh, or 1–2 tsp dried, dill
150ml double cream
150ml hot Sainsbury's Signature vegetable stock
2 egg yolks
grated zest of ½ lemon
salt and freshly ground black pepper
By Sainsbury's dill sprigs, to garnish
lemon wedges, to garnish

PER SERVING
820 cals
37.4g fat
17.4g saturated fat
3.9g total sugars
1.1g salt

PUT THE MINCED LAMB, spring onions, bacon, garlic and cinnamon in a food processor and blend until almost smooth.

WITH WET HANDS, SHAPE THE MIXTURE into 30–36 even-sized balls. Keep wetting your hands to avoid sticking.

PREHEAT THE OVEN TO 180°C/160°FAN/MARK 4. Heat the oil in a large frying pan and brown the meatballs in batches, then transfer to a shallow ovenproof dish. Discard any fat left in the frying pan, then pour in the wine and bring to the boil, scraping up any sediment from the bottom of the pan. Pour over the meatballs, cover and bake in the preheated oven for 1 hour.

REMOVE THE MEATBALLS FROM THE DISH, cover and keep warm. Pour the cooking liquid into a pan, bring to the boil and boil rapidly until reduced to about 300ml.

MEANWHILE, COOK THE TAGLIATELLE in a large pan of boiling water according to packet instructions. Drain and stir in the butter.

LOWER THE HEAT OF THE SAUCE and stir in the dill, cream and egg yolks. Stir over a gentle heat for about 10 minutes or until slightly thickened; do not allow to boil. Stir in the lemon zest, taste the sauce and adjust the seasoning.

TRANSFER THE MEATBALLS to warmed plates and spoon the sauce over them. Garnish with dill sprigs and lemon wedges and serve with the buttered pasta.

VARIATION

Use lean minced pork instead of lamb and tarragon in place of the dill.

Beef Stroganoff

PREPARATION TIME: 30 MINS | COOKING TIME: 1–1½ HOURS | SERVES 6 | ❄

A rich, hearty classic – beef, sweet peppers and garlic in a lightly spiced sauce finished with crème fraîche. This is comfort food at its best.

1.4kg Sainsbury's British stewing steak, diced
2 tbsp sunflower oil
200ml red wine
100ml hot Sainsbury's Signature beef stock
3 onions, sliced
3 red peppers, deseeded and sliced
3 garlic cloves, crushed
4 tbsp tomato purée
1 tbsp paprika
2 tbsp Dijon mustard
300g chestnut mushrooms, wiped and quartered
375g long grain rice, to serve
100ml Sainsbury's British crème fraîche
salt and freshly ground black pepper

SEASON THE STEWING STEAK with salt and pepper. Heat 1 tablespoon of oil over a high heat in a large frying pan and cook the beef for about 10 minutes until browned all over.

ADD THE RED WINE AND STOCK, bring to a simmer, then turn off the heat and set aside.

HEAT THE REMAINING OIL over a medium heat in a large pan and cook the onions, red peppers and garlic for about 5 minutes until softened. Stir in the tomato purée, paprika and mustard and season with salt and pepper. Add the beef and its cooking liquid to the pan and cook for 1–1½ hours until the beef is tender.

STIR THE MUSHROOMS INTO THE STROGANOFF and continue to cook for 15 minutes. Meanwhile, cook the rice according to packet instructions.

JUST BEFORE SERVING, stir the crème fraîche into the stroganoff. Serve spooned over the hot rice.

PER SERVING
690 cals
19.6g fat
8.4g saturated fat
9g total sugars
0.67g salt

VARIATION

In place of rice, spoon the stroganoff into hot, buttered baked potatoes.

Beef and Beer Stew with Buttery Mash

PREPARATION TIME: 25 MINS | COOKING TIME: 1¾ HOURS | SERVES 6 | ✳

This wonderfully dark, glossy stew is enriched with good strong beer and a hint of treacle. A spoonful of soft, buttery mash is the perfect accompaniment to soak up the delicious flavoursome juices. Serve with sautéed cabbage or another steamed green vegetable.

2 tbsp plain flour
1.1kg Sainsbury's braising beef, cut into large chunks, fat removed
4 celery sticks
a few thyme sprigs
2 bay leaves
25g beef dripping or lard
3 large onions, thinly sliced
450ml hot Sainsbury's Signature beef stock
450ml Sainsbury's Taste The Difference London Porter (or any strong beer)
3 tbsp black treacle
450g turnips, peeled and cut into large chunks
salt and freshly ground black pepper

For the buttery mash
900g floury potatoes, such as Sainsbury's King Edward
50g butter

PER SERVING
657 cals
28.8g fat
13.4g saturated fat
14.2g total sugars
0.76g salt

SEASON THE FLOUR WITH SALT AND PEPPER and use to coat the meat. Cut two 5cm lengths of celery. Tie in two bundles with the thyme and bay leaves. Cut the remaining celery into chunks.

PREHEAT THE OVEN TO 160°C/140°FAN/MARK 3. Heat the dripping or lard in a large flameproof casserole. Add half the meat and fry, turning, until lightly browned. Remove with a slotted spoon and fry the remainder; remove.

ADD THE ONIONS AND CELERY to the casserole and fry gently until softened. Return the meat to the casserole and add the herb bundles. Stir in the stock, beer and treacle, then add the turnips. Bring just to the boil, reduce the heat, cover with a lid and transfer to the oven. Cook for 1½ hours or until the meat and vegetables are tender.

ABOUT 30 MINUTES BEFORE THE END of the cooking time, make the mash. Peel the potatoes, then cut into even-sized pieces. Put them in a pan and cover with water. Bring to the boil, lower the heat and simmer for about 20 minutes until tender. Drain thoroughly and return to the pan. Add the butter and some seasoning and mash well until completely smooth.

DIVIDE THE STEW BETWEEN WARMED SERVING PLATES and serve with spoonfuls of creamy mash.

TIP
If you buy a head of celery with plenty of green leaves, chop the leaves finely and use to garnish the stew just before serving.

VARIATION
Instead of mashed potato, serve the stew with a creamy parsnip purée. Peel and cut 900g parsnips into 7.5cm lengths, then chop into even-sized pieces. Put into a pan and cover with water. Cover with a lid, bring to the boil then lower the heat and simmer for about 15 minutes until completely tender. Drain well, return to the pan and stir in 50ml double cream. Season well and mash until completely smooth.

POULTRY & MEAT

Pasta

Pasta in a Rich Provençal Sauce

PREPARATION TIME: 15 MINS | COOKING TIME: 40 MINS | SERVES 6

Here is a gutsy tomato sauce, flavoured generously with antipasti ingredients, such as marinated artichokes and capers. If you are cooking this dish for non-vegetarians and want to boost the flavour, stir in six chopped anchovy fillets at the end of the cooking time.

6 tbsp extra virgin olive oil
6 garlic cloves, finely chopped
200ml red wine
3 tbsp chopped rosemary
1 bay leaf
75g stoned black olives, sliced
3 tbsp Sainsbury's capers in brine, drained
2 x 400g cans plum tomatoes, roughly crushed
300g jar Sainsbury's Taste The Difference chargrilled artichokes in olive oil, drained and sliced
600g Sainsbury's conchiglie pasta
salt and freshly ground black pepper

HEAT THE OIL IN A LARGE PAN over a medium heat, add the garlic and cook for a few minutes until it softens. Pour in the red wine, increase the heat and boil rapidly until the wine has reduced by two thirds.

ADD THE ROSEMARY, bay leaf, olives, capers, tomatoes and artichokes and bring to a simmer. Season well with salt and pepper and cook for 20–30 minutes until thickened.

MEANWHILE, BRING A LARGE PAN OF SALTED WATER to the boil. Add the pasta and cook until al dente, or according to packet instructions. Drain, reserving about 2 tablespoons of the cooking water and return to the pan. Stir in the sauce, taste for seasoning and serve immediately.

PER SERVING
552 cals
19g fat
2.6g saturated fat
6.3g total sugars
1.5g salt

 TIP

This is a great way of using up any leftover roast chicken. Shred and stir into the sauce after cooking to warm through.

Fresh Pasta with Asparagus and Parmesan

PREPARATION TIME: 30 MINS, *plus resting* | COOKING TIME: 6–8 MINS | SERVES 4

Celebrate the asparagus season with this simple pasta dish. Although the recipe calls for fresh pasta, you can use dried instead, or vary the shape and try it with linguine instead.

225g Sainsbury's asparagus spears, trimmed
125g unsalted butter
2 garlic cloves, finely sliced
2 tsp salt
350g Sainsbury's fresh tagliatelle
4 tbsp shredded basil leaves
50g Sainsbury's grated Parmesan
salt and freshly ground pepper

PER SERVING
538 cals
31.8g fat
18.7g saturated fat
2.6g total sugars
0.7g salt

BRING A LARGE PAN OF WATER TO THE BOIL for the pasta. At the same time, steam the asparagus for 3 minutes until just tender; drain, and cut into 5cm lengths.

MEANWHILE, HEAT THE BUTTER with the garlic in a small pan and cook over a medium heat until it starts to turn brown. Immediately remove the garlic from the pan.

ADD 2 TEASPOONS OF SALT TO THE PASTA WATER. Plunge in the tagliatelle, return to the boil and cook for 2–3 minutes until al dente. Immediately drain and return the pasta to the pan. Add the asparagus, basil, butter and half the Parmesan and toss gently.

SERVE AT ONCE, sprinkled with the remaining Parmesan and plenty of black pepper.

VARIATION

This recipe can be adapted to whatever vegetables you have to hand. When the asparagus season is over, enjoy it with a mixture of green beans and peas, and later in the year, with sprouting broccoli.

Pasta Primavera

PREPARATION TIME: 25 MINS | COOKING TIME: 25 MINS | SERVES 4–6

Some of the spring vegetables – or *primavera* as they are known in Italy – in this colourful dish are cooked slowly until meltingly soft, sweet and buttery, while in contrast young asparagus, tiny carrots and sugar snap peas are cooked briefly to retain their fresh crispness.

175g By Sainsbury's fine asparagus spears
125g By Sainsbury's sugar snap peas, topped and tailed
1 red pepper
2 celery stalks
2 courgettes
6–8 spring onions, white parts only
225g carrots, preferably whole baby ones
25g butter
1 small onion, chopped
400g Sainsbury's tagliatelle
150ml double cream
150ml hot Sainsbury's Signature vegetable stock
4 tbsp freshly grated Parmesan
1 tbsp olive oil
4 tsp chopped chives
4 tsp chopped dill
salt and freshly ground black pepper

134

PASTA

PER SERVING
529 cals
23.5g fat
13g saturated fat
8.6g total sugars
0.47g salt

HALVE THE ASPARAGUS SPEARS and cook in boiling salted water for 3–4 minutes, adding the sugar snaps after 2 minutes so that both are cooked and just tender. Drain and refresh with cold water then drain again. Set aside.

USING A POTATO PEELER carefully pare the skin from the red pepper and discard, along with the core and seeds. Dice the red pepper, celery, courgettes and spring onions. If the carrots are tiny, baby ones, leave them whole; otherwise peel and slice finely.

MELT THE BUTTER IN A LARGE FRYING PAN. Add the onion and fry over a medium heat for 7–8 minutes until soft and golden. Add the red pepper, celery and carrots and cook for 12–15 minutes, stirring frequently, until the vegetables are tender and beginning to colour. Stir in the courgettes and spring onions and cook for 3–4 minutes.

COOK THE PASTA IN A LARGE PAN of boiling salted water until al dente, or according to packet instructions.

MEANWHILE, STIR THE CREAM AND STOCK into the vegetables and bring to a gentle boil. Allow to bubble, stirring frequently for a few minutes until it reduces by about one third. Stir in the asparagus and sugar snaps. Add the Parmesan and heat gently. Season with salt and pepper to taste.

DRAIN THE PASTA and transfer to a warmed large serving bowl. Toss with the oil to prevent sticking. Pour the sauce over the pasta and sprinkle with the herbs. Toss well and serve at once.

TIP

Because some of the vegetables are left whole it's best to balance the proportions with a good-sized pasta, and tagliatelle does this beautifully. If you prefer to use a pasta shape, choose a large one, such as rigatoni or spirali.

Macaroni Cheese

PREPARATION TIME: 15 MINS | COOKING TIME: 30 MINS | SERVES 4

This crowd-pleasing dish, containing just a handful of basic ingredients, is the perfect stand-by supper. 'Mac and cheese' as it's affectionately called by Americans, is essentially pasta in a cheese sauce, but here it's combined with mustard for a piquant flavour and topped with sliced tomatoes. You can also use other short pasta shapes, such as gigli, as pictured here.

400g Sainsbury's macaroni, gigli or other short pasta
50g butter
50g plain flour
600ml milk
100g By Sainsbury's British mature Cheddar, grated, plus extra to sprinkle
2 tbsp By Sainsbury's wholegrain mustard
4 tomatoes, sliced
salt and freshly ground black pepper

PER SERVING
730 cals
29.2g fat
16.8g saturated fat
12.2g total sugars
1.3g salt

COOK THE PASTA in a pan of boiling water until al dente.

MELT THE BUTTER IN A PAN over a medium heat and stir in the flour. Cook for 1–2 minutes until the mixture looks like a paste and starts to bubble in the pan. Take the pan off the heat and gradually add the milk, stirring all the time, to make a smooth sauce.

RETURN THE PAN TO THE HEAT and bring to the boil. Cook for 2–3 minutes. It's ready when you run your finger down the back of the spoon and it leaves a channel. Stir in three quarters of the cheese and all the mustard and season well with salt and pepper.

PREHEAT THE GRILL TO HOT. Drain the pasta, reserving about 2 tablespoons of the cooking water and return the pasta to the pan. Add the cheese sauce and stir well then spoon into four 600ml ovenproof dishes or one 2.5 litre ovenproof dish.

LAYER THE TOMATOES OVER THE TOP, then scatter over the remaining cheese. Grill until golden and bubbling.

137

PASTA

VARIATION

Omit the tomatoes and throw in a handful of frozen peas at the end of cooking the pasta. Drain well, then combine the pasta and sauce with chopped ham and parsley, cover with cheese and grill as above.

Fettucine with Gorgonzola and Spinach

PREPARATION TIME: 10 MINS | COOKING TIME: 10–15 MINS | SERVES 4–6

The rich and creamy flavour of this pasta sauce belies its few simple ingredients. Use tender young leaf spinach if possible. You can use larger spinach leaves, but you will need to remove their stalks and shred or roughly chop the leaves before cooking.

350g By Sainsbury's young leaf spinach
225g Sainsbury's creamy Gorgonzola, cut into small pieces
75ml milk
25g butter
450g Sainsbury's fettucine, tagliatelle or long fusilli
freshly ground black pepper
freshly grated nutmeg, to serve

PER SERVING
455 cals
18.1g fat
10.5g saturated fat
3g total sugars
1.9g salt

WASH THE SPINACH THOROUGHLY and remove any large stalks. Place in a large pan and cook, stirring, over a medium high heat for 2–3 minutes until wilted. There is no need to add extra water – the small amount clinging to the leaves after washing provides sufficient moisture. Drain well in a colander or sieve, pressing out any excess liquid.

PLACE THE GORGONZOLA IN A CLEAN PAN with the milk and butter. Heat gently, stirring, until melted to a creamy sauce. Stir in the drained spinach. Season to taste with pepper (you shouldn't need salt as Gorgonzola is quite salty).

COOK THE PASTA in a large pan of boiling salted water until al dente, or according to packet instructions.

DRAIN THE PASTA THOROUGHLY and add to the sauce. Toss well to mix. Serve at once, sprinkled with a little freshly grated nutmeg.

TIP

Gorgonzola is a soft blue-veined Italian cheese made from cow's milk. It comes in two varieties, creamy (*dolce*) and *piccante*. If you like a flavour with a bit of bite, choose *piccante*. If you prefer a softer taste, make this with the creamy variety.

VARIATION

Add 125g cooked smoked ham, cut into small dice or fine strips, to the sauce with the wilted spinach. As an alternative to Gorgonzola, make this dish with Dolcelatte, which will provide a milder, sweeter flavour.

Penne with Olives, Anchovy and Chilli

PREPARATION TIME: 5 MINS | COOKING TIME: 15 MINS | SERVES 4–6

Accompanying this pasta dish with a crisp leafy salad adds instant freshness to your meal and helps make up your daily quota of 'five-a-day'.

400g Sainsbury's penne
2 garlic cloves, thinly sliced
50g Sainsbury's canned anchovy fillets in olive oil
½ tsp dried chilli flakes
2 tbsp chopped parsley
225g stoned mixed black and green olives
4 tbsp extra virgin olive oil
2–3 tbsp Sainsbury's grated Parmesan, plus extra to serve
freshly ground black pepper

BRING A LARGE PAN OF SALTED WATER TO THE BOIL. Add the pasta and cook until al dente, or according to packet instructions.

PLACE THE GARLIC IN A PAN with the anchovies and their oil. Add the chilli flakes and cook over a fairly high heat for 2–3 minutes, stirring with a wooden spoon to break up the anchovies; do not allow the garlic to brown. Stir in the parsley and remove from the heat. Season with pepper to taste.

WHEN THE PASTA IS COOKED, drain and return to the pan, leaving a little cooking water still clinging to the pasta. Add the olives, olive oil and Parmesan. Toss well to coat the pasta. Serve immediately, topped with extra Parmesan.

PER SERVING
398 cals
16.8g fat
3.5g saturated fat
1.9g total sugars
2.3g salt

VARIATION
Add some steamed broccoli or cauliflower florets to the pasta and sauce with the olives.

Simple Prawn Pasta

PREPARATION TIME: 5 MINS | COOKING TIME: 15 MINS | SERVES 4

This recipe is a great one for summer, when courgettes are at their best. Take care not to overcook the garlic; it should fry gently in the butter just long enough to infuse it with a delicate flavour.

400g spirali pasta
knob of butter
1 garlic clove, sliced
250g raw peeled prawns
2 courgettes, grated
grated zest of ½ lemon
2–3 tbsp extra virgin
  olive oil
salt and freshly ground
  black pepper

PER SERVING
437 cals
9.9g fat
2.5g saturated fat
2.9g total sugars
0.3g salt

COOK THE PASTA IN A PAN OF BOILING SALTED WATER until al dente, or according to packet instructions.

WHILE THE PASTA IS COOKING, melt the butter in a pan over a low heat and add the garlic. Cook for 1 minute, but don't allow the garlic to brown. Turn off the heat. Add the prawns to the pan and allow to warm through in the heat of the pan, turning over every now and then until they're pink. Add the courgettes, lemon zest and season well with salt and pepper.

DRAIN THE PASTA reserving about 2 tablespoons of the cooking water and return the pasta to the pan. Add the prawn and courgette mixture, together with the olive oil. Toss everything together then divide between four bowls and serve immediately.

TIP

If you're using cooked prawns, add them to the pan of pasta when it's being mixed with the sauce and toss well so they warm through in the heat of the pan.

143

PASTA

Pasta with Mozzarella and Roasted Aubergine, Tomato and Garlic

PREPARATION TIME: 15 MINS | COOKING TIME: 40 MINS | SERVES 4

This recipe combines pasta with roasted vegetables and softened cloves of garlic. By cooking everything in the oven, the flavours are sweetened, and the garlic can be squeezed out of its pod at the end to give an extra mellow, slightly toffee-ish, savoury taste.

8 garlic cloves, unpeeled
1 red onion, roughly chopped
1 aubergine, roughly chopped
4 plum tomatoes, quartered
2 tbsp olive oil, plus extra to serve
4 thyme sprigs
400g pasta shapes
1 ball mozzarella, roughly torn into pieces
handful of basil leaves
salt and freshly ground black pepper

PREHEAT THE OVEN TO 200°C/180°FAN/MARK 6. Put the garlic, onion, aubergine and tomatoes in a large roasting tin. Drizzle over the oil and scatter over the thyme. Season well with salt and pepper and roast in the oven for 40 minutes until golden and starting to char at the edges. Remove the thyme sprigs.

COOK THE PASTA IN A PAN OF BOILING SALTED WATER until al dente, or according to packet instructions. Drain well and add the pasta to the roasting tin.

STIR THE MOZZARELLA INTO THE PASTA, drizzle over extra oil, add the basil and season well. Stir everything together well then divide among four bowls and serve.

PER SERVING
511 cals
14.2g fat
5.5g saturated fat
7.3g total sugars
0.37g salt

TIP

This is a great dish in which to use any slightly wizened, leftover vegetables from the bottom of the fridge. Courgettes, carrots and butternut squash would all work well.

Pasta Shells with Salmon and Dill

PREPARATION TIME: 15 MINS | COOKING TIME: 15–20 MINS | SERVES 4–6

The pleasure of this dish lies in the unusual combination of fresh and smoked salmon with their distinctive individual qualities. It is important to add the smoked salmon at the end of cooking in order to preserve its texture and flavour.

350g fresh salmon
   fillet, skinned
125g sliced smoked
   salmon
15g butter
1 onion, chopped
250ml dry white wine
2 tbsp wholegrain
   mustard
300ml half fat crème
   fraîche
2–3 tbsp chopped
   fresh dill
400g pasta shells
salt and freshly ground
   pepper
dill sprigs, to garnish
toasted pine nuts,
   to garnish

PER SERVING
487 cals
19.7g fat
8.1g saturated fat
3.9g total sugar
1.1g salt

146

PASTA

CUT THE SALMON FILLET INTO 2.5cm cubes. Cut the smoked salmon into strips. Set both aside.

MELT THE BUTTER IN A LARGE FRYING PAN. Add the onion and cook over a medium heat for about 7 minutes until soft and golden. Stir in the wine and mustard and bring to the boil. Cook for 5–7 minutes until reduced by half.

STIR IN THE CREAM AND CONTINUE COOKING for 1 minute, then lower the heat and add the fresh salmon to the pan. Cook gently for 2–3 minutes until the fish is firm. Stir in the dill and season with salt and pepper. Remove from the heat.

MEANWHILE, COOK THE PASTA in a large pan of boiling salted water until al dente, or according to packet instructions. Drain thoroughly then transfer to a warmed serving dish.

TO SERVE, GENTLY REHEAT THE SAUCE IF NECESSARY. Add to the pasta with the smoked salmon strips and toss lightly to mix. Serve at once, garnished with tiny sprigs of dill and sprinkled with toasted pine nuts.

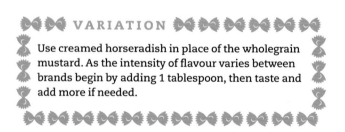

VARIATION

Use creamed horseradish in place of the wholegrain mustard. As the intensity of flavour varies between brands begin by adding 1 tablespoon, then taste and add more if needed.

Spaghetti Bolognese

PREPARATION TIME: 30 MINS | COOKING TIME: 1½ HOURS | SERVES 6 | ✳

Traditionally, this *ragù* (meat sauce) from Bologna in northern Italy is served over spaghetti, but it is also good spooned over hot jacket potatoes or used on pizza with mozzarella.

2 tbsp olive oil
1kg minced beef
2 onions, chopped
2 carrots, chopped
2 celery sticks, chopped
4 garlic cloves, chopped
100ml red wine
2 tbsp tomato purée
400g can chopped
    tomatoes
200ml hot beef stock
2 bay leaves
1 tbsp dried oregano
600g spaghetti
salt and freshly ground
    black pepper
grated Parmesan,
    to serve

PER SERVING
807 cals
32.7g fat
12.3g saturated fat
9.8g total sugars
0.57g salt

HEAT HALF THE OIL OVER A HIGH HEAT in a large pan and cook the mince for about 5 minutes until browned all over. Season well with salt and pepper and transfer to a plate.

HEAT THE REMAINING OIL OVER A MEDIUM HEAT in the same pan and cook the onions, carrots and celery for about 5 minutes until softened. Stir in the garlic.

POUR THE WINE INTO THE PAN and bring to a simmer to deglaze the pan. Add the tomato purée, chopped tomatoes, beef stock, bay leaves and oregano and add seasoning. Cover the pan and when it starts to simmer, turn the heat down low and cook for about 1½ hours until the beef is tender. Check the level of liquid in the sauce regularly and add a little boiling water if it looks dry. It should look thickened and saucy when cooked.

COOK THE SPAGHETTI in a large pan of boiling salted water until al dente, or according to packet instructions. Drain, divide between individual bowls and top with the sauce, handing around the grated Parmesan separately.

TIP

This sauce freezes brilliantly and is the perfect stand-by supper to have to hand. Make double and freeze half in a sealable container for up to 1 month.

Spaghetti alla Carbonara

PREPARATION TIME: 15 MINS | COOKING TIME: 7 MINS | SERVES 4–6

This classic Italian pasta dish – with its rich smoky bacon flavour and light, soft scrambled egg texture – is cooked as it should be, with the heat of the spaghetti setting the eggs to give a creamy sauce. If pecorino cheese is unobtainable, simple double the quantity of Parmesan.

125–150g smoked pancetta in slices
2 tbsp extra virgin olive oil
25g butter
1 garlic clove, halved
3 eggs
2 tbsp chopped fresh parsley
2 tbsp dry white wine
40g Parmesan, grated
40g pecorino cheese, grated
400g spaghetti
salt and freshly ground black pepper

PER SERVING
452 cals
20.5g fat
8g saturated fat
2.3g total sugar
1.1g salt

REMOVE THE RIND FROM THE PANCETTA, then cut into very thin strips. Heat the oil and butter in a heavy-based pan. Add the pancetta and garlic and cook over a medium heat for 3–4 minutes until the pancetta begins to crisp. Turn off the heat; discard the garlic.

MEANWHILE, IN A MIXING BOWL large enough to hold the cooked spaghetti later, beat the eggs with the parsley, wine and half of each of the cheeses. Season with salt and pepper.

COOK THE SPAGHETTI IN A LARGE PAN of boiling salted water until al dente, or according to packet instructions.

WHEN THE SPAGHETTI IS ALMOST COOKED, gently reheat the pancetta in the pan. Drain the spaghetti thoroughly, then immediately add to the egg mixture in the bowl with the pancetta. Toss well to cook the eggs until they are creamy. Add the remaining cheeses, toss lightly and serve at once.

TIP

Spaghetti with smoked salmon and scrambled eggs is prepared in a similar way. Omit the pancetta and garlic and instead add 125g smoked salmon strips to the egg mixture. Heat the butter and oil and add to the bowl with the pasta. Finish as above, adding the remaining cheese and tossing in the same way.

Pasta with Chorizo

PREPARATION TIME: 10 MINS | COOKING TIME: 50 MINS | SERVES 6 | ❄

Chorizo is a spicy Spanish sausage, liberally flavoured and coloured with paprika. It is available both raw by the piece, and cured, ready to slice and eat. If you use cured chorizo, cook it in the sauce for 5 minutes only. A robust red wine is the ideal accompaniment to this rustic dish.

2 tbsp olive oil
1 onion, finely chopped
2 garlic cloves, crushed
2 tbsp tomato purée
2 tbsp mild paprika
1 dried chilli, finely chopped
2 bay leaves
Leaves from 2 fresh thyme sprigs
2 tbsp fresh rosemary leaves
150ml red wine, such as Rioja or Tempranillo
400g can chopped tomatoes
450g raw chorizo sausage
600g pasta shapes, such as farfalle
salt and freshly ground black pepper
chopped parsley, to garnish

HEAT THE OIL IN A HEAVY-BASED PAN, add the onion and garlic and sauté for about 5 minutes or until softened. Add the tomato purée and paprika and cook for 2 minutes, stirring all the time.

ADD THE CHILLI, BAY LEAVES, THYME AND ROSEMARY. Pour in the wine and bring to the boil. Cook for 2 minutes, stirring. Add the tomatoes with their juice and bring to the boil again. Lower the heat and simmer gently for 30 minutes. Season generously with salt and pepper.

CUT THE CHORIZO SAUSAGE INTO THICK SLICES and pan-fry briefly until golden in a separate frying pan. Add to the sauce and cook for 15 minutes.

MEANWHILE BRING A LARGE PAN OF SALTED WATER to the boil. Add the pasta, bring back to the boil and stir once. Cook until al dente, or according to packet instructions. Drain thoroughly then divide between warmed individual serving bowls or turn into a large warmed serving bowl. Spoon the sauce on top of the pasta, sprinkle with plenty of chopped parsley and serve immediately.

PASTA

PER SERVING
673 cals
22.8g fat
8g saturated fat
7.5g total sugar
1.2g salt

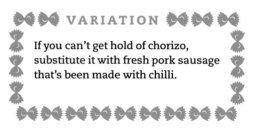

VARIATION

If you can't get hold of chorizo, substitute it with fresh pork sausage that's been made with chilli.

Tagliatelle with Chicken and Courgettes

PREPARATION TIME: 15 MINS | COOKING TIME: 35 MINS | SERVES 4

Buttery chicken is flavoured with garlic, ginger and chilli and tossed into pasta with melting courgettes and fresh herbs. Serve the dish on its own or accompanied by a crisp, mixed-leaf salad – such as rocket and chicory or radicchio and frisée – tossed in a light dressing.

4 boneless chicken breasts, skinned
3.5cm piece of fresh root ginger, peeled and grated
3 garlic cloves, finely chopped
3 red chillies, halved, deseeded and finely chopped
65g butter
2 small courgettes, thinly sliced
3 tbsp chopped fresh coriander or tarragon
1 tbsp chopped parsley
400g tagliatelle
salt and freshly ground pepper

PER SERVING
637 cals
17g fat
9.3g saturated fat
3g total sugars
0.5g salt

PREHEAT THE OVEN TO 190°C/170°FAN/MARK 5. Lay a large piece of foil on a baking sheet and arrange the chicken breasts in a single layer on top. Sprinkle with the ginger, garlic and chillies, dot with 25g of the butter and season with salt and pepper.

FOLD OVER THE EDGES OF THE FOIL TIGHTLY to form a parcel. Bake in the oven for 30 minutes or until the chicken is tender and cooked through.

MEANWHILE, MELT THE REMAINING BUTTER in a large frying pan. Add the courgettes and cook over a medium heat, stirring frequently, for 4–5 minutes until tender and just beginning to brown. Stir in the herbs and cook briefly. Remove from the heat.

ABOUT 5 MINUTES BEFORE THE CHICKEN WILL BE READY, cook the pasta in a large pan of boiling salted water until al dente, or according to packet instructions.

WHEN THE CHICKEN IS COOKED, carefully lift out of the parcel, retaining the juices in the foil. Cut the chicken into slices or cubes and return to the foil.

DRAIN THE PASTA AND RETURN TO THE PAN. Add the chicken with its juice and the courgette and herb mixture. Toss lightly to mix. Adjust the seasoning to taste and serve at once.

155

PASTA

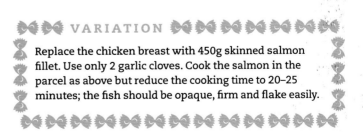

VARIATION

Replace the chicken breast with 450g skinned salmon fillet. Use only 2 garlic cloves. Cook the salmon in the parcel as above but reduce the cooking time to 20–25 minutes; the fish should be opaque, firm and flake easily.

Rigatoni Baked with Spicy Sausage

PREPARATION TIME: 15–20 MINS | COOKING TIME: 30–35 MINS | SERVES 4–6

You can use any good-quality spicy sausage for this recipe, but – if at all possible – buy Italian- or Sicilian-style uncooked sausages. Prepare the sauce in advance if you wish, but don't toss with the pasta until ready for the oven, otherwise the pasta will become soggy.

3 tbsp extra virgin olive oil
350g uncooked spicy sausages
1 onion, chopped
2 garlic cloves, chopped
90ml dry white wine
2 tbsp chopped oregano
1 tbsp chopped parsley
2 x 400g cans plum tomatoes
12 black olives, stoned and sliced
5 sun-dried tomatoes, diced
400g rigatoni
butter, for greasing
175g mozzarella (preferably smoked), diced
50g Parmesan, in one piece
salt and freshly ground black pepper

PER SERVING
600 cals
28.8g fat
11.3 g saturated fat
6.9g total sugars
1.9g salt

HEAT 1 TABLESPOON OF THE OIL IN A LARGE FRYING PAN, then add the sausages. Fry on a medium heat for 4–5 minutes, turning frequently, until lightly browned. Transfer to a plate and cut into slices. Set aside.

ADD THE REMAINING OIL TO THE FRYING PAN. Stir in the onion and garlic and cook over a medium heat for 5 minutes until softened but not browned. Return the sliced sausage to the pan and add the wine and herbs. Increase the heat and cook for 3–4 minutes until about two thirds of the wine has evaporated.

STIR IN THE CANNED TOMATOES AND THEIR JUICE, breaking them up with a wooden spoon. Add the olives and sun-dried tomatoes. Cook, uncovered, over a medium heat for 15–20 minutes until the tomatoes are pulp-like; do not reduce the sauce too much. Season with salt and pepper, to taste.

MEANWHILE, PREHEAT THE OVEN TO 200°C/180° FAN/ MARK 6. Cook the rigatoni in a large pan of boiling salted water until almost al dente, or for about 2 minutes less than the packet instructions. Drain thoroughly.

BUTTER A BAKING DISH OR ROASTING TIN large enough to hold the pasta and sauce, about 2.5 litres. Transfer the pasta to the dish and toss with the sauce. Scatter the mozzarella over the rigatoni. Using a potato peeler, 'shave' the Parmesan over the top. Bake near the top of the oven for about 15 minutes until piping hot. Serve at once.

157

PASTA

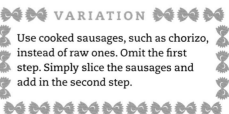

VARIATION

Use cooked sausages, such as chorizo, instead of raw ones. Omit the first step. Simply slice the sausages and add in the second step.

Vegetable Lasagne

PREPARATION TIME: 1 HOUR | COOKING TIME: 40 MINS | SERVES 6 | ❄ *(before baking)*

This is a crowd-pleasing dish whether you're cooking for vegetarians or meat-lovers. The layers of pasta are sandwiched with a rich Mediterranean vegetable filling, then finished with an indulgent cream cheese topping.

4 red, orange or yellow peppers
1 large aubergine
5 tbsp extra virgin olive oil, plus extra for greasing
1 large onion, chopped
4 garlic cloves, thinly sliced
5 tbsp red wine or hot vegetable stock
3 tbsp chopped flat-leaf parsley
4 tbsp tomato purée
1 large courgette
12 Sainsbury's lasagne sheets
salt and freshly ground black pepper

For the topping
300g cream cheese
3 eggs
2 tbsp dry white breadcrumbs
2 tbsp freshly grated Parmesan

PER SERVING
574 cals
34.3g fat
16.6g saturated fat
13.3g total sugars
1.3g salt

PREHEAT THE GRILL TO HOT. Grill the whole peppers, turning from time to time, until the skins are blackened and blistered all over. This will take about 20 minutes. Allow to cool slightly, then, over a bowl to catch the juices, remove the skins. Chop the flesh, discarding the seeds, and set aside with the juices.

MEANWHILE, CUT THE AUBERGINES INTO 1cm dice. Place in a colander, rinse, then sprinkle liberally with salt. Leave for 20 minutes, to extract the bitter juices. Rinse again, then blanch in boiling water for 1 minute; drain well.

HEAT 3 TABLESPOONS OF THE OIL IN A LARGE PAN. Add the onion and cook, stirring frequently, for about 8 minutes until soft and golden. Add the garlic and cook for a further 2 minutes. Add the wine and allow to bubble for 1 minute, then stir in the aubergine, parsley and tomato purée. Cover and cook over a medium heat for 15–20 minutes, stirring frequently. Add the courgette and simmer for 5 minutes more. Remove from the heat and stir in the grilled peppers. Season.

PREHEAT THE OVEN TO 190°C/170°FAN/MARK 5. Cook the lasagne sheets in a large pan of boiling salted water until al dente, or according to packet instructions. Drain, then drop into a bowl of cold water with 2 tablespoons of oil added to prevent the sheets from sticking. Drain again and lay on a clean tea towel.

OIL A BAKING DISH, MEASURING ABOUT 25 x 18 x 8cm. Spread one third of the filling over the base then cover with a layer of pasta, trimming to fit the dish as necessary. Repeat twice more.

TO MAKE THE TOPPING, place the cream cheese in a bowl, add the eggs and beat well. Season with salt and pepper. Spoon over the lasagne and spread evenly. Sprinkle with the breadcrumbs and Parmesan, then bake for about 35–40 minutes until heated through and lightly browned on top.

Seafood Lasagne

PREPARATION TIME: 30 MINS | COOKING TIME: 30–40 MINS | SERVES 6

Fish and fennel are a complementary pairing of flavours and here they're combined in a crowd-pleasing lasagne. The topping couldn't be easier – simply beat together mascarpone, eggs and cheese and spoon over the top. On baking, it sets into a thick cheesy topping covering the fish and pasta layers beneath.

1 tbsp olive oil
25g butter
1 onion, finely chopped
1 celery stick, chopped
1 fennel bulb, chopped
1 tsp fennel seeds
1–2 tbsp Pernod
400g can chopped
    tomatoes
100ml hot fish stock
1 tbsp chopped parsley
6–8 lasagne sheets
450g seafood mix, such
    as chopped squid,
    prawns and mussels
250g tub mascarpone
2 eggs
50g pecorino cheese,
    freshly grated

PER SERVING
416 cals
29g fat
16.5g saturated fat
5.3g total sugars
0.7g salt

HEAT THE OIL AND BUTTER IN A PAN until the butter has melted. Add the onion, celery and fennel and cook for 10 minutes until softened.

STIR IN THE FENNEL SEEDS AND PERNOD and bring to the boil to cook off the alcohol. Add the chopped tomatoes and stock and simmer for 10 minutes to thicken. Stir in the parsley, then turn off the heat.

COOK THE LASAGNE SHEETS in a large pan of boiling water, then drain well. Preheat the oven to 190°C/170°Fan/Mark 5.

LAYER HALF THE SEAFOOD IN A LARGE OVENPROOF DISH. Spoon over half the tomato sauce, then cover with a layer of the lasagne sheets. Repeat.

BEAT THE MASCARPONE, EGGS and half the grated pecorino cheese in a bowl and season well with salt and pepper. Spoon on top of the lasagne and cover with the remaining cheese. Bake in the oven for 30 minutes until the top is golden.

TIP

Replace the seafood with chunks of raw fish, such as salmon or line-caught cod.

Vegetarian & Vegetable Sides

Chinese-style Vegetable Noodles

PREPARATION TIME: 10 MINS | COOKING TIME: 20 MINS | SERVES 4

This easy-to-cook home-made version of sweet-and-sour noodles can be ready and on the table, quicker than the time it takes to call for a takeaway. The natural flavours of the vegetables are enhanced by zingy citrus flavours and delicate spices.

250g Sainsbury's free range fresh egg noodles
1 tbsp sunflower oil
1 medium onion, thickly sliced
50g Sainsbury's Fairtrade cashew nuts
2 celery sticks, sliced on the diagonal
2 carrots, halved lengthways and sliced thickly on the diagonal
2 garlic cloves, chopped
3cm piece fresh root ginger, peeled and cut into matchsticks
pinch of chilli flakes
1 star anise
1 green pepper, thickly sliced
1 red pepper, thickly sliced
225g can water chestnuts, halved
2 tbsp rice wine vinegar
2 tbsp dry sherry
1 tbsp caster sugar
juice of 1 lime
juice of 2 oranges
1 tbsp cornflour
½ tbsp sesame oil
1 tbsp soy sauce
200g Sainsbury's mangetout, halved
4 spring onions, thinly sliced on the diagonal
salt and freshly ground black pepper

COOK THE NOODLES in a large pan of boiling water, according to the timings on the packet, then drain.

HEAT THE OIL IN A LARGE LIDDED WOK or frying pan over a high heat and cook the onion for 5–8 minutes until starting to turn golden. Add the cashew nuts, celery, carrots, garlic and ginger and cook for a further 2–3 minutes until tinged with brown. Scatter over the chilli flakes, star anise, peppers and water chestnuts. Add 2 tablespoons of cold water. Cover with a lid and cook for 5–8 minutes until the vegetables are just tender but still have a slight bite.

MEANWHILE, IN A SMALL BOWL COMBINE THE VINEGAR, mirin, sherry, sugar, lime juice, orange juice, cornflour, sesame oil and soy sauce. Season well with salt and pepper then pour the sauce over the vegetables. Add the mangetout, cover and simmer for about 3 minutes until the sauce has thickened and is coating all the vegetables.

ADD THE DRAINED NOODLES TO THE PAN and toss with the vegetables. Serve spooned into warmed bowls, topped with the sliced spring onions.

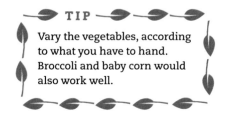

TIP

Vary the vegetables, according to what you have to hand. Broccoli and baby corn would also work well.

PER SERVING
615 cals
23.5g fat
4.7g saturated fat
26.4g total sugars
0.4g salt

Split Pea Dal with Buttered Naan

PREPARATION TIME: 15 MINS, *plus soaking* | COOKING TIME: 1¼ HOURS | SERVES 4 | ❄

A steaming bowl of *chana dal* served with naan or chapati is pure Indian comfort food.

300g Sainsbury's dried yellow split peas (or *chana dal*)

1.2 litres hot Sainsbury's Signature vegetable stock

2 tbsp sunflower or olive oil

25g butter

3 tsp coriander seeds, crushed

1½ tsp cumin seeds, crushed

1 large onion, finely chopped

4 garlic cloves, chopped

1 red and 1 green chilli, thinly sliced

5cm piece fresh root ginger, peeled and finely chopped

zest and juice of 1 lemon

25g fresh coriander, roughly chopped

150g young leaf spinach

salt and freshly ground black pepper

For the naan

25g Sainsbury's English salted butter, at room temperature

large pinch of chilli powder

1 tbsp finely chopped coriander

2 Sainsbury's Taste The Difference plain naan breads

WASH THE SPLIT PEAS and leave to soak in cold water for 8 hours or overnight.

DRAIN THE SPLIT PEAS and place in a large pan, cover with the stock and place over a medium heat. Bring to the boil, then reduce the heat and simmer for 15 minutes, skimming off any foam with a wooden spoon.

IN A LARGE FRYING PAN, heat the oil and butter then add the coriander and cumin seeds, onion, garlic, chillies and ginger and cook for 5 minutes until the onion is soft. Stir into the split peas and cover. Reduce the heat to a gentle simmer and cook for about 1 hour until the peas are very soft.

ABOUT 5 MINUTES BEFORE THE END of cooking, check the seasoning and add salt and pepper if necessary, then stir in the lemon zest and juice, fresh coriander and spinach leaves. Allow to heat through.

FOR THE NAAN, PREHEAT THE GRILL TO MEDIUM. Mix together the butter, chilli powder and coriander. Sprinkle both sides of each naan with water and place them under the grill, flat-side up, for 2 minutes. Turn, spread with the spiced butter and grill for a further 1–2 minutes until golden and bubbling. Serve straight away with the dal.

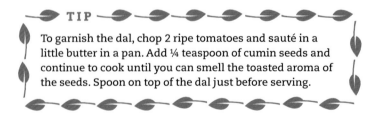

TIP

To garnish the dal, chop 2 ripe tomatoes and sauté in a little butter in a pan. Add ¼ teaspoon of cumin seeds and continue to cook until you can smell the toasted aroma of the seeds. Spoon on top of the dal just before serving.

VEGETARIAN & VEGETABLE SIDES

PER SERVING
681 cals
25.9g fat
9.4g saturated fat
4.8g total sugar
1.7g salt

Mushroom and Ale Casserole with Thyme Dumplings

PREPARATION TIME: 25 MINS, *plus 20 mins soaking* | COOKING TIME: 30–35 MINS | SERVES 4

If you're searching for comfort food for the colder months, look no further than a hearty casserole with dumplings. Choose a paler-coloured ale, as darker varieties can be too bitter once cooked.

15g Sainsbury's dried porcini mushrooms
2 tbsp olive oil
16 shallots, halved
3 carrots, peeled and cut into chunks
3 celery sticks, sliced
25g butter
350g Sainsbury's closed cup chestnut mushrooms, halved or quartered
300ml Sainsbury's Taste The Difference Suffolk blond ale
2 tbsp chopped fresh thyme
2 bay leaves
1 tbsp wholegrain mustard
3 tbsp mushroom ketchup
300ml hot Sainsbury's Signature vegetable stock
2 tsp cornflour
salt and freshly ground black pepper

For the dumplings
200g self-raising flour
1 tsp English mustard powder
100g salted butter, chilled
1 tbsp chopped fresh thyme
1 tbsp finely chopped parsley

PER SERVING
570 cals
33.3g fat
17.3g saturated fat
11.1g total sugar
1.8g salt

PLACE THE PORCINI IN A BOWL, cover with 100ml boiling water and leave to soak for 20 minutes. Remove the mushrooms, drain briefly and roughly chop. Strain the soaking liquid through a sieve lined with kitchen paper and set aside.

HEAT THE OIL OVER A MEDIUM–HIGH HEAT in a large pan, add the shallots, carrots and celery and cook for 5 minutes until tinged brown. Remove from the pan and set aside. Add the butter to the pan, increase the heat, add the porcini and chestnut mushrooms, season well and cook for 5 minutes until golden.

RETURN THE VEGETABLES to the pan and pour in the ale. Boil rapidly for a few minutes until reduced by half. Add the herbs, mustard, mushroom ketchup, stock and the reserved mushroom liquor. Mix the cornflour with 2 tablespoons of cold water in a small bowl until smooth, then add to the casserole and stir. Cover and simmer over a low heat for 20 minutes.

MAKE THE DUMPLINGS. Sieve the flour and mustard powder into a large bowl and season well with salt and pepper. Coarsely grate the cold butter into the flour, dipping it into the flour to prevent sticking. Add the herbs and rub in the butter until the texture resembles coarse breadcrumbs. Add 6–8 tablespoons of cold water a tablespoon at a time, mixing with a table knife to combine, until you have a soft, lightly sticky dough. Cut into 8 portions and shape into balls. Drop onto the casserole, cover, and continue to cook for 10–15 minutes or until the dumplings have a light springiness.

VARIATION

For spiced cheese-flavoured dumplings, stir 25g finely grated Cheddar and 1 tablespoon of paprika into the flour mixture before adding the water.

Thai Green Curry with Pan-fried Tofu

PREPARATION TIME: 15 MINS | COOKING TIME: 30 MINS | SERVES 4

Making your own Thai curry paste from scratch requires patience, so you might think it's not worth the effort, especially when you taste this delicious recipe, which simply uses a good-quality bought curry paste.

3 tbsp sunflower or groundnut oil
200g shallots, sliced
3 garlic cloves, chopped
3 tbsp Sainsbury's Thai green curry paste
2 fresh or dried kaffir lime leaves
1 tsp palm sugar or light muscovado sugar
400g can coconut milk
150ml hot Sainsbury's Signature vegetable stock
2 tsp Thai fish sauce (omit for vegetarians)
600g By Sainsbury's King Edward potatoes (or other waxy variety), peeled and cut into 3cm chunks
2 carrots, peeled, halved lengthways and cut thickly on the diagonal
2 peppers, roughly chopped
150g green beans, halved
150g By Sainsbury's baby corn
250g firm tofu, cut into 3cm cubes
250g pak choi, leaves separated
3 tbsp roughly chopped fresh coriander, plus extra to garnish
lime wedges, to serve

PER SERVING
562 cals
32.9g fat
16.8g saturated fat
15.5g total sugar
1.3g salt

HEAT 2 TABLESPOONS OF THE OIL in a large pan over a high heat, add the shallots and garlic and cook for 5 minutes until golden. Stir in the curry paste, lime leaves and sugar and cook for a minute until aromatic. Pour in the coconut milk, stock and fish sauce (if using) and bring to the boil.

ADD THE POTATOES, carrots, peppers and green beans. Scatter the baby corn on top and simmer for 20 minutes until the potatoes are tender.

ABOUT 10 MINUTES BEFORE THE END of the cooking time, heat the remaining oil in a frying pan over a high heat, add the tofu and fry until golden. Stir into the curry with the pak choi and coriander and leave for 2 minutes until the leaves have wilted. Serve the curry scattered with coriander and with some lime wedges alongside to squeeze over for a little extra zing.

TIP
For added crunch, scatter over 25g roughly chopped salted peanuts before serving.

Moorish Potato and Cauliflower Stew

PREPARATION TIME: 20 MINS | COOKING TIME: 30–35 MINS | SERVES 4–6

In this fragrant and aromatic stew, spices turn two humble vegetables into a really special dish. Crush your potatoes a little on the plate to soak up all the vibrant broth, and use a spoon to scoop up every last drop.

3 tbsp olive oil
1 large onion, roughly chopped
2 garlic cloves, sliced
600g By Sainsbury's baby potatoes, scrubbed and halved or quartered if large
2 tsp coriander seeds, ground
2 tbsp tomato purée
5cm piece cinnamon stick
large pinch of saffron
1 large celery stick, sliced
1 medium cauliflower, about 500g, broken into florets
75g sultanas
400g can Sainsbury's butterbeans, drained
700ml hot Sainsbury's Signature vegetable stock
3 large fresh tomatoes, peeled, seeded and chopped
40g flaked almonds, toasted
salt and freshly ground black pepper

PER SERVING
302 cals
11g fat
1.5g saturated fat
15.7g total sugar
0.88g salt

HEAT THE OIL in a large heavy-based pan over a medium heat and cook the onion, garlic and potatoes for 4–5 minutes until tinged brown. Add the coriander seeds and tomato purée and cook for a further minute, stirring.

ADD THE CINNAMON, saffron, celery, cauliflower, sultanas and butterbeans, stir, then pour over the stock.

CHECK THE SEASONING then cover and simmer for 20–30 minutes until the potatoes are tender.

BEFORE SERVING, stir in the tomatoes, then divide between the bowls and scatter each serving with toasted flaked almonds.

> VARIATION
> Use 400g canned chickpeas, drained, in place of the butterbeans.

173

VEGETARIAN & VEGETABLE SIDES

Hearty Bean Stew with Herbs

PREPARATION TIME: 15 MINS | COOKING TIME: 45 MINS | SERVES 6 | ❄

Made from storecupboard ingredients and a handful of vegetables, this is perfect for wintery weekends when you need something warm and nourishing. The beans give the dish body, while the chilli and herbs provide a kick of spice and flavour.

50g butter
2 celery sticks, chopped
3 carrots, chopped
2 onions, chopped
1 potato, peeled and roughly chopped
1 orange pepper, deseeded and chopped
2 litres hot Sainsbury's Signature vegetable stock
1 bay leaf
1 tbsp fresh or dried thyme
½ tsp crushed chilli flakes
400g can Sainsbury's haricot beans, drained and rinsed
400g can Sainsbury's kidney beans, drained and rinsed
400g can Sainsbury's chickpeas, drained and rinsed
500g creamed tomatoes or passata
1 courgette, chopped
3 tbsp finely chopped flat-leaf parsley
sea salt and freshly ground black pepper

PER SERVING
357 cals
9.1g fat
4.7g saturated fat
10.4g total sugar
2.1g salt

HEAT THE BUTTER IN A LARGE PAN over a medium heat and lightly brown the celery, carrots and onions for 10 minutes.

ADD THE POTATO, pepper, stock, bay leaf, thyme, chilli, beans, chickpeas and creamed tomatoes or passata. Season well with salt and pepper then cover and simmer for 30 minutes.

STIR IN THE COURGETTE AND PARSLEY, cover again and continue to cook for 5 minutes until the courgette is tender.

TIP

Serve with garlic and herb croutes. Mash 25g butter with ½ crushed garlic clove and 1–2 tablespoons of freshly chopped parsley. Toast slices of baguette and, while still warm, spread over the butter.

Tortilla

PREPARATION TIME: 20 MINS | COOKING TIME: 35 MINS | SERVES 4

The literal translation of this Spanish favourite is 'little cake', although apart from the eggs used it bears little relation to baking. It is a one-pan treat of vegetables and soft-cooked egg. In its most simple form, it is made with layers of potatoes and served as a *tapa* – light bite.

4 tbsp vegetable or olive oil
1 onion, finely chopped
600g potatoes, such as Sainsbury's Charlotte potatoes, chopped
1 red pepper, deseeded and chopped
1 green pepper, deseeded and chopped
4 Sainsbury's free range woodland eggs
salt and freshly ground black pepper

PER SERVING
332 cals
18.3g fat
3.1g saturated fat
6.5g total sugars
0.25g salt

HEAT THE OIL IN A 20CM OVENPROOF FRYING PAN and gently cook the onions and potatoes over a low heat for about 20 minutes until softened but not golden.

ADD THE CHOPPED PEPPERS and continue to cook for a further 5 minutes until tender.

PREHEAT THE GRILL TO HOT. Beat the eggs in a bowl and season well. Pour over the vegetables, tipping the pan so that the raw egg runs into all the holes. Cook over a low–medium heat until the base is golden, about 5 minutes.

PUT THE PAN UNDER THE GRILL and cook until just golden. Watch it carefully and do not allow it to overcook; a tortilla should be served just firm on the outside but still slightly wobbly in the middle. Serve immediately.

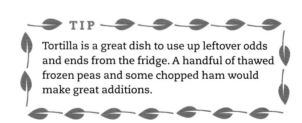

TIP

Tortilla is a great dish to use up leftover odds and ends from the fridge. A handful of thawed frozen peas and some chopped ham would make great additions.

Red Pepper Falafel Bake

PREPARATION TIME: 25 MINS | COOKING TIME: 20–30 MINS | SERVES 4–6

Filled with the classic flavours of cumin, coriander and tahini, this falafel-inspired dish is a versatile alternative to making the patties. Serve it warm or chilled with the yoghurty dip and some crisp salad leaves.

a little vegetable or olive oil for greasing
½ tbsp coriander seeds
1 tsp cumin seeds
125g roasted red peppers in brine, drained
400g can Sainsbury's chickpeas, drained
1 garlic clove, crushed
2 tbsp tahini paste
1½ tbsp extra virgin olive oil
juice of ½ lemon
1 tbsp toasted sesame seeds
25g fresh white breadcrumbs
50g spring onions, finely sliced
2 tbsp roughly chopped fresh coriander
salt and freshly ground black pepper

For the yoghurt dip
15cm piece cucumber, halved and seeded
150g By Sainsbury's natural yoghurt
1 tbsp tahini paste
2 tbsp chopped dill
squeeze of lemon juice

PER SERVING
194 cals
12.5g fat
2.1g saturated fat
4.5g total sugar
0.54g salt

PREHEAT THE OVEN TO 190°C/170°FAN/MARK 5. Lightly oil a 19–20cm diameter tin. Toast the coriander and cumin seeds in a small frying pan over a medium heat until aromatic, then transfer to a pestle and mortar and grind until coarse. Pat the peppers dry on kitchen paper, then cut into 1cm dice.

PUT THREE-QUARTERS OF THE CHICKPEAS, the garlic, tahini, olive oil and lemon juice into a food processor and pulse until coarse. Scoop the mixture into a bowl and mix in the ground spices, peppers, sesame seeds, breadcrumbs, spring onions and fresh coriander, reserving a tablespoon of peppers, sesame seeds and spring onions for garnish. Season well with salt and pepper.

SPOON EVERYTHING INTO THE TIN, smooth the surface and scatter with the reserved chickpeas, peppers, sesame seeds and spring onions. Cook in the oven for 20–30 minutes until golden.

MEANWHILE MAKE THE YOGHURT DIP. Coarsely grate the cucumber then squeeze out the juice between your hands. Transfer the cucumber to a bowl and combine with the yoghurt, tahini, dill and some lemon juice to taste.

TO SERVE, RUN A KNIFE ROUND THE EDGE OF THE BAKE then upturn onto a plate. Immediately upturn the right way up onto a serving plate. Serve the dip alongside.

TIP
Any leftovers can be spread on toasted bread for a quick and easy snack.

179

VEGETARIAN & VEGETABLE SIDES

Vegetable Ragout with Cheese Polenta Topping

PREPARATION TIME: 40 MINS, *plus cooling* | **COOKING TIME: 30 MINS** | **SERVES 6–8** | ❄

This rich, thick stew of leeks, tomatoes, aubergines and chickpeas, topped with a golden crust of cheesy polenta, will appeal to meat eaters and vegetarians alike.

700g aubergines
450g Sainsbury's Taste The Difference jubilee large vine tomatoes
150ml olive oil
450g leeks, thickly sliced
2 garlic cloves, crushed
150ml dry white wine
400g can Sainsbury's chopped tomatoes
2 tbsp sun-dried tomato paste
400g can chickpeas, drained
a sprig of rosemary
1 tbsp balsamic vinegar

For the polenta topping
185g quick-cook polenta
50g Sainsbury's Swiss Gruyère, grated
3 tbsp Sainsbury's grated Parmesan
salt and freshly ground black pepper

PER SERVING
356 cals
19.8g fat
4.6g saturated fat
7.2g total sugar
0.3g salt

CUT THE AUBERGINES INTO LARGE CHUNKS, place in a colander and sprinkle with salt. Leave to drain for 30 minutes.

PLUNGE THE TOMATOES INTO BOILING WATER for 30 seconds. Refresh under cold water and slip off the skins. Halve, squeeze out the seeds and discard. Cut the tomatoes into quarters.

HEAT 2 TABLESPOONS OF OLIVE OIL in a large pan and add the leeks and garlic. Fry over a medium heat for 5 minutes until softened and beginning to brown but not disintegrated.

ADD THE FRESH TOMATOES AND WINE and cook over a high heat for about 7 minutes until the tomatoes have softened and the wine has evaporated. Stir in the canned tomatoes, tomato paste and chickpeas.

RINSE THE AUBERGINES THOROUGHLY, then pat dry with kitchen paper. Heat the remaining olive oil in a frying pan and fry the aubergines over a high heat until browning. Stir into the leek and tomato mixture. Pour the ragout into a large shallow ovenproof dish and allow to cool.

PREHEAT THE OVEN TO 200°C/180°FAN/MARK 6. To make the topping, bring 800ml water to the boil in a large heavy-based pan with 1 teaspoon of salt. Sprinkle in the polenta, stirring all the time. Cook, stirring, for 5–10 minutes until thick. Stir in the Gruyère, 2 tablespoons of Parmesan and plenty of salt and pepper. Spread in a shallow tin to a thickness of 2cm and allow to cool. When cold, stamp into rounds with a 4cm cutter.

LAY THE POLENTA IN OVERLAPPING CIRCLES on top of the vegetable ragout. Sprinkle with the remaining Parmesan and bake for about 30 minutes until golden brown and heated through.

TIP
This is perfect hot buffet dish and can be cooked ahead for larger numbers.

Pine Nut, Fennel and Parmesan Risotto

PREPARATION TIME: 15 MINS | COOKING TIME: 30–40 MINS | SERVES 6

You can experiment with different flavours in this risotto by adding other vegetables at the end: try stirring in some steamed asparagus, fresh peas or stir-fried courgette along with the rocket.

3 tbsp olive oil
2 onions, chopped
4 Sainsbury's fennel heads, trimmed and sliced thinly
3 garlic cloves, chopped
2 litres hot vegetable stock
500g Arborio rice
2 bay leaves
250ml white wine
125g Sainsbury's toasted pine nuts
100g Sainsbury's grated Parmesan, plus extra to serve
25g butter
25g fresh dill, chopped
100g Sainsbury's wild rocket
salt and freshly ground black pepper

HEAT THE OIL IN A LARGE SAUCEPAN over a medium heat and cook the onions, fennel and garlic for about 10–15 minutes until softened but not coloured.

POUR THE STOCK INTO A SEPARATE PAN and bring to a gentle simmer.

ADD THE RICE TO THE SOFTENED VEGETABLES and stir, cooking it for 1–2 minutes until heated through. Add the bay leaves and wine and continue to cook, stirring all the time, until most of the wine has been absorbed. Start to add the stock, a ladleful at a time, and continue to stir until most of the liquid has been absorbed before adding another.

ONCE THE LAST LADLE OF STOCK HAS BEEN ADDED, stir in the pine nuts, Parmesan, butter, dill and rocket. Taste for seasoning and serve with extra Parmesan grated on top.

PER SERVING
669 cals
30.3g fat
7.6g saturated fat
4.3g total sugar
0.46g salt

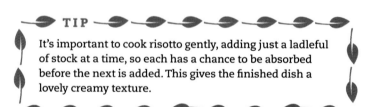

TIP

It's important to cook risotto gently, adding just a ladleful of stock at a time, so each has a chance to be absorbed before the next is added. This gives the finished dish a lovely creamy texture.

Creamy Leek Tart

PREPARATION TIME: 30 MINS, *plus chilling* | COOKING TIME: 35–40 MINS | SERVES 8

A delicious creamy tart filled with soft, melting leeks. It makes a wonderful picnic dish, but can equally be served warm as a starter or with a tomato salad for lunch.

250g plain white flour
1 tsp salt
125g butter, softened
1 large Sainsbury's free range woodland egg yolk

For the filling
50g butter
1.4kg leeks, trimmed and sliced
3 Sainsbury's free range woodland egg yolks
300ml Sainsbury's crème fraîche
freshly grated nutmeg
sea salt and freshly ground black pepper

PER SERVING
480 cals
37g fat
22g saturated fat
5g total sugar
1g salt

TO MAKE THE PASTRY, sift the flour and salt onto a sheet of greaseproof paper. Put the butter and egg yolk in a food processor and blend until smooth. Add the flour and work until just combined. Turn out onto a lightly floured work surface and knead gently until smooth. Form into a ball, flatten and wrap in plastic film. Chill in the fridge for at least 30 minutes. Allow to come to room temperature before rolling out.

MEANWHILE, PREPARE THE FILLING. Melt the butter in a large pan, add the leeks and stir to coat in the butter. Add 2 tablespoons of water, cover and cook gently, stirring occasionally, for about 20 minutes until very soft but not coloured. Season well with salt and pepper. Set aside to cool.

PREHEAT THE OVEN TO 200°C/180°FAN/MARK 6. Roll out the pastry thinly on a lightly floured surface and use to line a 25cm loose-bottomed flan tin. Chill for 20 minutes, then lightly prick the base with a fork.

CUT A SQUARE OF BAKING PARCHMENT large enough to cover the pastry case. Scrunch it up into a ball, then pull apart and lay on top of the tart tin. Fill with baking beans and bake in the oven for 12–15 minutes. Remove the baking beans and continue to bake for about 5 minutes, or until the pastry feels dry to the touch.

BEAT THE EGG YOLKS AND CRÈME FRAÎCHE TOGETHER, adding a little freshly grated nutmeg. Spread the leeks around the pastry case and pour over the egg mixture.

REDUCE THE OVEN TEMPERATURE TO 190°C /170°Fan/Mark 5 and bake for a further 20–25 minutes until the tart is set and browned on top. Serve warm or cold.

184

VARIATION
Stir 125g chopped Parma ham into the crème fraîche mixture. Sprinkle 125g grated Gruyère over the top of the tart before cooking (see picture).

TIP
This method of baking the pastry before adding the filling is known as 'baking blind'. If you don't have any ceramic baking beans, use uncooked rice or dried beans instead. Once used, store in a jar, label and reuse again in place of baking beans.

Red Cabbage Slaw

PREPARATION TIME: 20 MINS, *plus standing* | **SERVES 4–6**

Nothing tastes quite as good as homemade coleslaw and this recipe is particularly rich and creamy. It is good served as part of a selection of salads, and is an ideal side dish to accompany barbecued food.

225g red cabbage, cored
2 medium carrots,
    peeled
50g raw beetroot, peeled
1 red onion, peeled
2 apples
1 garlic clove, crushed
50g Sainsbury's pecan
    nuts, toasted and
    roughly chopped

For the dressing
150ml By Sainsbury's
    lighter mayonnaise
4 tbsp natural yoghurt
1 tbsp orange juice
1 tbsp red wine vinegar
2 tbsp chopped By
    Sainsbury's chives
salt and freshly ground
    black pepper

COARSELY GRATE OR SHRED THE CABBAGE, carrots and beetroot, using a food processor fitted with a coarse grater if possible, and place in a large bowl. Finely slice the onion. Quarter, core and grate the apples. Add to the bowl with the garlic and pecan nuts.

TO MAKE THE DRESSING, beat together the mayonnaise, yoghurt, orange juice and vinegar. Stir in the chives and season with salt and pepper.

SPOON THE DRESSING OVER THE VEGETABLES and stir well until thoroughly mixed. Cover and set aside for 30 minutes at a cool room temperature to allow the flavours to develop. Toss the salad before serving.

PER SERVING
181 cals
13.3g fat
1.2g saturated fat
10.9g total sugar
0.69g salt

TIP
As the flavours develop on standing, the salad is best prepared in advance.

VEGETARIAN & VEGETABLE SIDES

Roasted Mushrooms with Lemon and Garlic Oil

PREPARATION TIME: 5 MINS, *plus 3 days standing* | COOKING TIME: 20–25 MINS | SERVES 4–6

You will need to prepare the oil infusion 3 days in advance.

2 garlic cloves
½ tsp sea salt
finely pared peel
    of 1 lemon
150ml Sainsbury's
    olive oil
8 By Sainsbury's large
    flat field mushrooms,
    each about 12cm
    across
2 tbsp chopped parsley
salt and freshly ground
    black pepper
lemon wedges, to serve

PER SERVING
176 cals
18.7g fat
2.7g saturated fat
0.2g total sugar
0.3g salt

CRUSH THE GARLIC AND SALT TOGETHER with a pestle and mortar or on a chopping board and place in a sterilised jar. Add the lemon peel and pour in the oil. Shake well to ensure that the garlic and lemon are covered by the oil and seal the jar. Refrigerate for 3 days.

WHEN READY TO PREPARE THE MUSHROOMS, preheat the oven to 220°C/200°Fan/Mark 7. Place the mushrooms, stalk-side up, in a shallow roasting tin, or two separate ones, in which they fit closely together.

DRIZZLE TWO THIRDS OF THE OIL LIBERALLY over the mushrooms and bake in the oven for 15 minutes. Turn the mushrooms over and baste with more oil. Bake for a further 5–10 minutes until the mushrooms are tender and brown, basting occasionally.

ARRANGE THE MUSHROOMS on a large warmed serving plate and scatter over the chopped parsley. Season with salt and pepper. Serve at once, with lemon wedges and accompanied by any remaining infused oil.

189

TIP
To barbecue the mushrooms, place them, stalk-side up, on a doubled piece of foil, pour over the infused oil and seal the foil. Cook over the coals for 20 minutes and serve straight from the parcels.

VEGETARIAN & VEGETABLE SIDES

Swede and Carrots with Mustard Seeds and Ginger

PREPARATION TIME: 20 MINS | COOKING TIME: 15 MINS | SERVES 4

Swede is often a much maligned vegetable, yet it has a distinctive flavour that is enhanced by herbs, spices and aromatic ingredients. Swede and carrots go well together, and the addition of mustard seeds and ginger gives the combination a more interesting dimension.

450g swede, peeled and cut into small dice
450g carrots, peeled and thinly sliced
25g butter
1 tsp By Sainsbury's mustard seeds
2 pieces Sainsbury's preserved stem ginger in syrup, drained and finely chopped
salt and freshly ground black pepper

PER SERVING
123 cals
6.2g fat
3.4g saturated fat
15.6g total sugar
0.2g salt

COOK THE SWEDE AND CARROTS in a pan of boiling salted water until tender.

MELT THE BUTTER in a small heavy-based pan. Add the mustard seeds and heat gently until the seeds begin to pop. Add the chopped ginger and cook for 1 minute over a low heat.

DRAIN THE COOKED SWEDE AND CARROTS thoroughly, then mash together. Season liberally with freshly ground black pepper and stir in half of the mustard and ginger mixture.

TRANSFER THE MASHED SWEDE and carrots to a warmed serving dish and drizzle the remaining mustard and ginger mixture over the top. Serve at once.

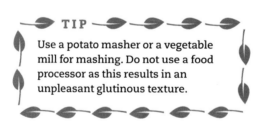

TIP
Use a potato masher or a vegetable mill for mashing. Do not use a food processor as this results in an unpleasant glutinous texture.

190

Parsnips in a Lime Glaze

PREPARATION TIME: 5 MINS | COOKING TIME: 15 MINS | SERVES 4

Here the tang of lime is used to enhance the flavour of sweet parsnips. If possible, use young parsnips as they are likely to be more tender. The sharp glaze can be used with any sweet root vegetable to excellent effect – try it with sweet potatoes or carrots.

675g Sainsbury's Taste The Difference heritage baby parsnips, peeled
50g butter
25g light muscovado sugar
grated zest and juice of 1 lime
salt and freshly ground black pepper
freshly chopped chives, to garnish

PER SERVING
224 cals
12.1g fat
6.8g saturated fat
15.3g total sugar
0.24g salt

TRIM THE TOPS AND ROOTS OF THE PARSNIPS. Cut in half lengthways (if using older, tougher parsnips cut into quarters and remove the woody core). Place in a pan of boiling salted water and cook for 5 minutes.

MELT THE BUTTER IN A LARGE PAN together with the sugar. Add the lime juice and heat gently, stirring, to dissolve the sugar.

DRAIN THE PARSNIPS THOROUGHLY in a colander, then add to the lime mixture in the pan. Toss and cook over a medium heat, shaking the pan frequently, for about 10 minutes until golden brown. Season with salt and pepper.

TRANSFER TO A WARMED SERVING DISH and garnish with the lime zest and chives.

 VARIATION

Use carrots or turnips instead of parsnips. A handful of walnuts tossed in towards the end of the cooking time adds a delicious crunch.

VEGETARIAN & VEGETABLE SIDES

Potato and Mushroom Gratin

PREPARATION TIME: 5 MINS | COOKING TIME: 20 MINS | SERVES 2

This is a satisfying supper dish for two that is very easy to knock together and can be ready and on the table within half an hour. Serve with a crispy leaf salad.

250g small new potatoes, halved (unless they are very small)
2 tbsp olive oil
1 small onion, chopped
125g By Sainsbury's closed cup mushrooms, left whole if small; halved or sliced if large
125g By Sainsbury's British mild Cheddar, grated
freshly ground black pepper

COOK THE POTATOES in salted boiling water until tender, about 15 minutes. Drain thoroughly.

MEANWHILE, HEAT THE OLIVE OIL in a frying pan over a low heat and add the onion. Cook gently, stirring frequently, until softened. Add the mushrooms to the pan, stir and cook for 2–3 minutes. Preheat the grill to medium–high.

TRANSFER THE ONION AND MUSHROOMS to a flameproof gratin dish and stir in the potatoes. Season with pepper (it won't need salt) and sprinkle the cheese all over the surface. Grill until the cheese is bubbling, then serve immediately.

PER SERVING
468 cals
33.6g fat
15.3g saturated fat
3.7g total sugar
1.1g salt

 VARIATION

For meat-eaters you could cook 125g chopped rindless bacon with the onion until crisp. Cook together slowly over a low heat, stirring often, taking care that the onion doesn't burn.

VEGETARIAN & VEGETABLE SIDES

Indian-style Potatoes and Cauliflower

PREPARATION TIME: 15 MINS | COOKING TIME: 15 MINS | SERVES 4

Known as *aloo gobi*, this is a popular side dish which is very simple to make. The main ingredients, cauliflower and potatoes are flavoured with a handful of typical Indian seasonings. If you are serving it as an accompaniment to a very hot dish, you might prefer to reduce the chilli or leave it out altogether.

700g Sainsbury's King Edwards potatoes (or other waxy variety), peeled and cut into large chunks
6 tbsp vegetable oil
1 large onion, finely chopped
7.5cm piece fresh root ginger, finely chopped
1 garlic clove, crushed
1 hot green chilli, finely sliced (seeds retained for a hotter dish)
1½ tsp By Sainsbury's cumin seeds
1½ tsp By Sainsbury's ground coriander
¾ tsp By Sainsbury's ground turmeric
700g cauliflower, cut into small florets
100ml hot vegetable stock
salt and freshly ground black pepper

PER SERVING
231 cals
12.6 g fat
1.6g saturated fat
4.7g total sugars
trace salt

PLACE THE POTATOES IN A PAN with enough salted water to cover, bring to the boil and boil for 5 minutes. Drain.

MEANWHILE, HEAT THE VEGETABLE OIL in a large frying pan. Add the onion and ginger and cook over a medium heat until the onion is golden brown but not burnt. Add the garlic, chilli and spices and cook for 2 minutes, stirring all the time.

ADD THE POTATOES AND CAULIFLOWER, stirring to coat them in the spice mixture. Season with salt and pepper and stir in the vegetable stock. Cover with a lid and cook gently over a medium heat for about 10 minutes, or until the potatoes and cauliflower are tender. Check occasionally during cooking, adding a little extra water if necessary to prevent sticking. Don't overcook the vegetables; they should retain their shape.

VARIATION

Omit the chilli and replace the stock with 150ml coconut milk then stir in 1 tablespoon of chopped coriander at the end.

197

VEGETARIAN & VEGETABLE SIDES

Stir-fried Tenderstem Broccoli and Mangetout

PREPARATION TIME: 5 MINS | COOKING TIME: 10 MINS | SERVES 4

Tenderstem broccoli, so called because of its edible tender stem, has been developed by crossing broccoli with Chinese kale. Here it's used in a speedy vegetable side dish that is packed with goodness and can be ready and on the table in 15 minutes.

200g Sainsbury's tenderstem broccoli
1tbsp vegetable oil
1 red chilli, finely sliced
1 garlic clove, finely sliced
2cm piece fresh root ginger, finely chopped
100g Sainsbury's mangetout
1 tsp sesame oil
1 tbsp soy sauce, plus extra to serve
15g flaked almonds, toasted

CUT ANY THICK STEMS OF BROCCOLI in half lengthways. Heat the oil in a wok and add the broccoli, stir-frying and tossing around the pan for about 5 minutes until golden on the edges.

ADD THE CHILLI, GARLIC, GINGER and mangetout and cook for 1 minute, then add 1 tablespoon of water. Cover with a lid and allow the vegetables to steam for a few minutes.

ADD THE SESAME OIL, soy sauce and flaked almonds and toss everything together again. Spoon onto a plate and drizzle with extra soy sauce to serve.

PER SERVING
81 cals
6.1g fat
0.7g saturated fat
1.9g total sugars
0.69g salt

TIP

For a main meal, serve this dish on top of egg-fried rice or throw in a handful of cooked prawns at the end of cooking and serve with noodles.

Leeks in a Simple Cheese Sauce

PREPARATION TIME: 5 MINS | COOKING TIME: 20 MINS | SERVES 6

This recipe is very easy to make and is great if you want to have something prepared ahead that can be finished off quickly just before serving (see TIP below).

500g small/medium leeks
25g butter
1tsp olive oil
150ml hot Sainsbury's Signature vegetable stock
150g crème fraîche
100g Sainsbury's Swiss Gruyère, grated
1 tsp Dijon mustard
salt and freshly ground black pepper

PER SERVING
223 cals
20g fat
12.6g saturated fat
2.3g total sugars
0.49g salt

CUT EACH LEEK EQUALLY INTO FOUR LENGTHS. Melt the butter in a pan and add the oil. When the butter has stopped foaming, add the leeks in batches to the pan and sauté gently to brown. Pour in the stock, cover and simmer gently for 10 minutes until tender and still whole.

PREHEAT THE GRILL. Lift the leeks into an ovenproof dish, leaving behind the stock. Add the crème fraîche, 75g of the Gruyère and the mustard to the stock and stir together, seasoning well. Bring to the boil, then spoon over the leeks. Sprinkle over the remaining grated cheese and grill until golden.

TIP

To make ahead, prepare the leeks, cool and chill for up to 2 days, keeping the stock separate. Take the leeks out of the fridge and allow to come to room temperature. Spoon into the ovenproof dish and pour over 100ml of water. Cover tightly with foil and put in a preheated oven at 200°C/180°Fan/Mark 6 for 20–30 minutes until heated through. Remove the foil and preheat the grill, then heat the sauce as above and complete the recipe.

Baby Roast Potatoes with Shallots and Thyme

PREPARATION TIME: 15 MINS | COOKING TIME: 40 MINS | SERVES 4

This makes an ideal accompaniment to a Sunday roast as the potatoes can be cooked underneath the joint in the oven. You can also use soft herbs, such as parsley and chives, in place of the thyme. Don't add them until the end of cooking though, otherwise they'll wilt and lose their flavour in the heat of the oven.

8 shallots, peeled
  (see TIP, below) and
  halved if large
500g By Sainsbury's
  baby potatoes,
  scrubbed and halved
  or quartered if large
2 tbsp olive oil
a few thyme sprigs
salt and freshly ground
  black pepper

PREHEAT THE OVEN TO 200°C/180°FAN/MARK 6. Put the shallots in a roasting tin with the new potatoes. Drizzle over the oil and season well with salt and pepper. Roast in the oven for 20 minutes.

TAKE THE TIN OUT OF THE OVEN and give it a good shake. Add the thyme and continue to roast for a further 20 minutes until the potatoes and shallots are cooked through.

PER SERVING
155 cals
6g fat
0.9g saturated fat
4.2g total sugars
trace salt

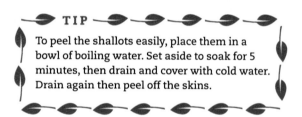

TIP

To peel the shallots easily, place them in a bowl of boiling water. Set aside to soak for 5 minutes, then drain and cover with cold water. Drain again then peel off the skins.

Garlic Potato Cake

PREPARATION TIME: 20 MINS | COOKING TIME: 35–40 MINS | SERVES 6

Thin potato sticks are tossed with garlic and thyme and cooked in a frying pan to a golden, crisp cake – rather like a robust rösti. It is a good accompaniment to serve with roast meats and chicken dishes.

700g By Sainsbury's
  Maris Piper potatoes
  (or another floury
  variety)
6 garlic cloves, crushed
2 tbsp chopped thyme
  leaves
125g unsalted butter
salt and freshly ground
  black pepper

PER SERVING
364 cals
26.3g fat
16.9g saturated fat
1g total sugars
trace salt

PREHEAT THE OVEN TO 200°C/180°FAN/MARK 6. Peel the potatoes and immerse in a bowl of cold water to get rid of any starch. Drain, slice thinly, then cut into thin sticks, a little thicker than matchsticks. Place in a bowl (don't worry if they brown a little – this won't be apparent once cooked). Add the garlic and thyme and toss well. Season liberally with salt and pepper.

SLOWLY MELT THE BUTTER in a small pan, then skim off any white residue or foam from the surface to leave what is known as clarified butter. Keep warm.

POUR 2 TABLESPOONS OF THE CLARIFIED BUTTER into a heavy-based 25cm non-stick, ovenproof frying pan. Transfer the potato sticks to the pan, spread evenly and press down firmly to form a 'cake'. Pour over the remaining butter.

PLACE THE PAN OVER A MEDIUM HEAT and cook for 5 minutes or until the underside begins to turn golden brown. To check, carefully lift up the edge of the potato cake with a palette knife.

PRESS THE POTATOES DOWN FIRMLY once more and cover with a lid or a buttered sheet of foil. Bake in the oven for 25–30 minutes, or until the potatoes are tender when pierced with a sharp knife and the underside is a deep golden brown.

LIFT OFF THE FOIL, place a lid or plate on top of the potato cake, invert onto the lid and slide back into the pan. Cook over a medium heat for 5 minutes, or until golden and crisp. Loosen the cake with a palette knife so that it moves freely.

PLACE A WARMED SERVING PLATE OVER THE PAN and invert the potato cake on to the plate. Serve immediately.

205

VEGETARIAN & VEGETABLE SIDES

Cakes, Biscuits & Bread

Honey and Yoghurt Muffins

PREPARATION TIME: 15 MINS | COOKING TIME: 17–20 MINS | MAKES 12 | ❋

American-style muffins rise considerably during baking to produce a wonderfully craggy texture. It's important not to completely blend the wet and dry ingredients together otherwise the finished muffin will be heavy and stodgy. This honey and yoghurt version has a healthy addition of oatmeal and sultanas – perfect for breakfast!

225g plain flour
1½ tsp baking powder
1 tsp bicarbonate
    of soda
pinch of salt
½ tsp ground mixed
    spice
¼ tsp ground nutmeg
50g medium oatmeal,
    plus extra to finish
75g light muscovado
    sugar
75g sultanas
zest of 1 orange
50g unsalted butter
225g Sainsbury's
    Greek-style yoghurt
125ml milk
1 medium egg
3 tbsp By Sainsbury's
    clear honey

PREHEAT THE OVEN TO 200°C/180°FAN/MARK 6. Line a 12-hole deep muffin tin with paper muffin cases.

SIFT THE FLOUR, baking powder, bicarbonate of soda, salt, mixed spice and nutmeg into a bowl. Stir in the oatmeal and sugar, breaking down any lumps, then add the sultanas and orange zest. Make a well in the middle of the mixture.

MELT THE BUTTER and leave to cool slightly. Mix the yoghurt and milk together in a bowl, then beat in the egg, butter and honey.

POUR THE MIXTURE INTO THE WELL and quickly stir the wet and dry ingredients together until just blended; do not overmix.

DIVIDE THE MIXTURE EQUALLY between the paper cases. Sprinkle with oatmeal and bake for 17–20 minutes until well risen and just firm to the touch.

REMOVE FROM THE OVEN and leave in the tins for 5 minutes, then transfer to a wire rack. Serve warm or cold.

PER SERVING
203 cals
6.3g fat
3.4g saturated fat
15.5g total sugars
0.6g salt

VARIATION

For chocolate banana muffins, omit the honey, sultanas and orange zest. Mash 1 small ripe banana and mix with 125g melted plain chocolate. Add to the muffin mixture after the liquids, blending until rippled with colour.

Apple and Blackberry Scone Pie

PREPARATION TIME: 15 MINS | COOKING TIME: 50 MINS | SERVES 6 | ❄

Here the classic combination of tangy apples and fresh blackberries excels once again. The pastry that envelops the fruit filling is made from a simple scone mixture and flavoured with just a hint of cinnamon. Serve just warm with spoonfuls of half-fat crème fraîche as a moreish teatime treat – or pudding if you prefer.

1 Sainsbury's Bramley cooking apple, about 175g, peeled, cored and thinly sliced
25g caster sugar
¼ tsp ground cloves
150g Sainsbury's blackberries
2 tsp cornflour
200g self-raising flour
pinch of salt
½ tsp ground cinnamon
1 tsp baking powder
75g By Sainsbury's unsalted butter, cut into small pieces
25g medium oatmeal, plus extra to finish
50g light muscovado sugar
90–100ml milk, plus extra to brush
demerara sugar, to finish

PER SERVING
300 cals
11.8g fat
7.2g saturated fat
17g total sugars
0.7g salt

PREHEAT THE OVEN TO 200°C/180°FAN/MARK 6. Lightly grease a 20cm springform tin. Place the apple in a bowl with the sugar, cloves, 75g blackberries and cornflour. Toss gently to mix.

SIFT THE FLOUR, SALT, CINNAMON AND BAKING POWDER together and place in a food processor. Add the butter and work until the mixture resembles breadcrumbs. Add the oatmeal and sugar. Add most of the milk and process briefly to a soft dough, adding the remaining milk if the mixture is too dry.

ON A FLOURED SURFACE, roll out two thirds of the dough to a round about 23cm in diameter. Use to line the tin, so that the dough comes about 2.5cm up the sides. Pile the apple and blackberry mixture into the centre and brush the edges of the dough with a little milk.

ROLL OUT THE REMAINING DOUGH to a 19–20cm round and lay over the filling, pressing the edges gently together to secure. Brush the top with milk. Sprinkle with oatmeal and muscovado sugar and bake for 30 minutes until well risen and golden. Reduce the oven temperature to 160°C/140°Fan/Mark 3.

SCATTER THE SCONE WITH THE REMAINING BLACKBERRIES and sprinkle with more oatmeal and muscovado sugar. Return to the oven for a further 20 minutes, covering with foil if the scone appears to be overbrowning. Leave in the tin for 5 minutes then transfer to a wire rack to cool.

VARIATION

Use pears (preferably the cooking variety) in place of apple. Frozen blackberries can be used, but they will result in a slightly wetter consistency.

Shortbread Biscuits

PREPARATION TIME: 20 MINS, *plus chilling* | **COOKING TIME: 13–15 MINS** | **MAKES 35**

You don't need any special equipment for this recipe – just a bowl, a spoon and a baking sheet. Leave the butter out overnight so it's soft when you make the biscuits, or soften it from the fridge by putting it in the microwave on the lowest setting. Check it at 10-second intervals until it's soft and easily spreadable, but take care that none of the butter melts. This way it will be easy to cream it with the sugar and make a soft dough when mixed with the flour.

150g By Sainsbury's
    unsalted butter,
    softened
75g Sainsbury's
    Fairtrade golden
    caster sugar, plus
    extra to sprinkle
200g plain flour
25g cornflour

PER SERVING
62 cals
3.6g fat
2.2g saturated fat
2.2g total sugars
trace salt

PREHEAT THE OVEN TO 180°C/160°FAN/MARK 4. Using a wooden spoon or an electric whisk, cream the butter and sugar together in a bowl for 3–4 minutes until pale and creamy.

SIFT HALF THE FLOUR INTO THE BOWL and work in with a wooden spoon. Add the remaining flour and the cornflour and do the same again. Bring the mixture together with your hands and knead lightly to make a smooth dough. Wrap in greaseproof paper and chill for 10 minutes.

ROLL OUT THE DOUGH on a lightly floured board and cut out 35 rounds using a 5cm fluted cutter. Prick all over with a fork.

BAKE ON A BAKING SHEET FOR 13–15 minutes until just golden. Sprinkle with a little caster sugar, then transfer to a wire rack to cool. Store in an airtight container for up to 5 days.

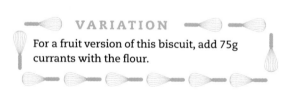

VARIATION

For a fruit version of this biscuit, add 75g currants with the flour.

Date and Banana Loaf

PREPARATION TIME: 20 MINS | COOKING TIME: 1¼–1½ HOURS | MAKES 8–10 SLICES | ❊

This simple, homely tea bread has a beautifully moist texture and a distinctive banana flavour. A layer of puréed dates provides added interest. To ring the changes, use other dried fruits, such as figs, prunes and apricots, in place of the dates.

250g stoned dried dates
grated zest and juice
    of 1 lemon
2 ripe Sainsbury's
    Fairtrade bananas
175g unsalted butter,
    softened
175g caster sugar
3 eggs
225g self-raising flour
½ tsp baking powder

PER SERVING
396 cals
16.8g fat
9.7g saturated fat
40g total sugars
0.58g salt

PREHEAT THE OVEN TO 160°C/140°FAN/MARK 3. Grease and line a 900g loaf tin with a paper loaf-tin liner.

SET ASIDE 4 DATES. Place the remainder in a small heavy-based saucepan and add the lemon zest and juice and 90ml water. Bring to the boil, reduce the heat and simmer gently for 5 minutes until the dates are soft and pulpy. Purée the mixture in a food processor or blender until smooth (alternatively mash together in a bowl using a fork).

MASH THE BANANAS until completely smooth. Cream the butter and sugar together in a bowl until pale and fluffy. Add the banana purée and the eggs. Sift the flour and baking powder into the bowl and beat until thoroughly combined.

SPOON HALF THE BANANA MIXTURE into the prepared loaf tin and level the surface. Spread the date purée over the surface, then cover with the remaining banana mixture.

CUT THE RESERVED DATES into thin lengths and scatter them over the surface. Bake for 1–1¼ hours until well risen and firm to the touch. Leave in the tin for 15 minutes, then transfer to a wire rack to cool. Store in an airtight container, wrapped in cling film, for up to 1 week.

CAKES, BISCUITS & BREAD

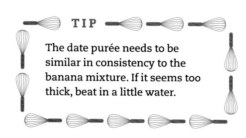

TIP

The date purée needs to be similar in consistency to the banana mixture. If it seems too thick, beat in a little water.

Spiced Finger Biscuits

PREPARATION TIME: 12 MINS | COOKING TIME: 15 MINS | MAKES 24–30

Crisp and light with a slightly chewy centre, these simple finger biscuits are made with a touch of spice for added flavour. Serve with coffee or as an accompaniment to creamy desserts.

2 egg whites
2 tsp cornflour
½ tsp ground cardamom
½ tsp By Sainsbury's
   ground ginger
125g caster sugar
75g ground almonds
icing sugar, to dust

PER SERVING
34 cals
1.4g fat
0.4g saturated fat
4.3g total sugars
trace salt

PREHEAT THE OVEN TO 180°C/160°FAN/MARK 4. Line two large baking sheets with non-stick baking parchment.

WHISK THE EGG WHITES in a bowl until stiff but not dry. Sift the cornflour and spices over the beaten egg white, add the sugar and ground almonds and gently stir the ingredients together to form a light sticky paste.

PLACE THE MIXTURE IN A LARGE PIPING BAG fitted with a 1cm plain nozzle. Pipe 7cm finger lengths onto the baking sheet, spacing them slightly apart. If you don't have a piping bag, spoon walnut-sized pieces of the mixture onto the baking sheet, spaced well apart. Bake for 12 minutes until crisp and golden. Transfer the sheets of baking parchment to a wire rack and allow to cool. Carefully peel the finger biscuits away from the paper. Dust with icing sugar before serving.

TIP

Chill any leftover egg yolks for up to three days in a sealable container and use to glaze the Chicken pie on page 96. Alternatively freeze for up to 1 month. Beat in a pinch of salt for savoury recipes or a sprinkling of sugar for sweet recipes so they are still useable, otherwise they thicken on freezing. Don't forget to label them.

Double Chocolate Cookies

PREPARATION TIME: 15 MINS | COOKING TIME: 12–15 MINS | MAKES 30 | ❄

Chunky, crumbly and rich with chocolate, these delicious biscuits closely resemble home-baked American-style cookies. This quick, simple recipe, with its generous proportions of dark and white chocolate, is guaranteed to appeal to all chocolate lovers.

125g Sainsbury's white Belgian cooking chocolate
125g Sainsbury's Taste The Difference dark Belgian cooking chocolate
125g unsalted butter, softened
125g caster sugar
2 eggs
1 tsp vanilla extract
125g porridge oats
150g plain flour
½ tsp baking powder

PER SERVING
130 cals
6.8g fat
3.8g saturated fat
9g total sugars
trace salt

PREHEAT THE OVEN TO 180°C/160°FAN/ MARK 4. Lightly grease two baking sheets. Chop the white and plain chocolate into small chunks, each no larger than 1cm in diameter.

PUT THE BUTTER AND SUGAR IN A BOWL and beat until creamy and pale. Add the eggs, vanilla extract and oats. Sift the flour and baking powder into the bowl, then add the chocolate. Mix until evenly combined.

TAKE A GENEROUS TEASPOON OF THE MIXTURE, about the size of an apricot, roll into a ball and place on the prepared baking sheet. Repeat with the remaining mixture, spacing the balls well apart to allow room for spreading. Flatten slightly with the back of a fork.

BAKE FOR ABOUT 15 MINUTES until risen and turning golden around the edges. Turn the baking sheet round halfway through if one side is browning more than the other.

LEAVE ON THE BAKING SHEETS for 5 minutes then transfer to a wire rack to cool. Store in an airtight tin for up to 1 week.

218

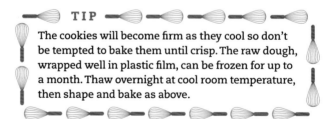

TIP
The cookies will become firm as they cool so don't be tempted to bake them until crisp. The raw dough, wrapped well in plastic film, can be frozen for up to a month. Thaw overnight at cool room temperature, then shape and bake as above.

Moist Fruit Cake with Glacé Fruits

PREPARATION TIME: 20 MINS, *plus cooling* | **COOKING TIME: 1–1¼ HOURS** | **SERVES 12** | ❄

An impressive arrangement of glacé cherries and almonds tops this exceptionally moist fruit cake, in which the dried fruits are first simmered in a buttery syrup to plump and sweeten them.

200g Sainsbury's dried apple, roughly chopped
300g Sainsbury's mixed dried fruit
200g molasses sugar
175g unsalted butter
275ml cold black tea
350g self-raising flour
1 tsp baking powder
1 tbsp ground mixed spice
1 medium egg
2 tbsp black treacle
5 balls stem ginger in syrup, drained and chopped

To decorate
6–8 tbsp By Sainsbury's apricot jam
100g glacé cherries, halved
100g blanched almonds

PREHEAT THE OVEN TO 160°C/140°FAN/MARK 3. Grease and line a deep 23cm round tin with greaseproof paper.

PLACE THE CHOPPED DRIED APPLE IN A PAN with the mixed dried fruit, molasses sugar, butter and tea. Bring to the boil, reduce the heat and simmer gently for 5 minutes. Remove from the heat and leave to cool completely.

SIFT THE FLOUR, baking powder and mixed spice into a bowl. Add the cooled fruit mixture, egg, treacle, stem ginger and any liquid and beat well until the ingredients are evenly combined.

TURN THE CAKE MIXTURE INTO THE PREPARED TIN and level the surface. Bake for 1–1¼ hours, or until a skewer inserted in the centre comes out clean. Leave in the tin for 15 minutes then transfer to a wire rack to cool.

TO DECORATE THE CAKE, heat the apricot jam in a small saucepan with 1–2 tablespoons of water until melted. Spoon the mixture into a sieve resting over a bowl and push it through with a wooden spoon, leaving behind any bits of apricot. Brush a little of the glaze over the cake. Arrange the cherries over the cake, spaced apart, then fill in with the almonds. Brush with the remaining glaze.

220

PER SERVING
467 cals
17.8g fat
8.5g saturated fat
51.5g total sugars
0.47g salt

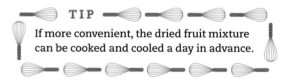

TIP
If more convenient, the dried fruit mixture can be cooked and cooled a day in advance.

VARIATION
For a more everyday fruit cake, omit the glacé fruit topping. Instead, generously sprinkle the top of the cake with demerara sugar before baking.

Chocolate Fudge Cake

PREPARATION TIME: 50 MINS, *plus cooling* | COOKING TIME: 25 MINS | MAKES 8–10 SLICES | ❄

A perfect cake for a celebration or for afternoon tea. The dark, rich chocolate sponge is sandwiched together with a filling of whipped cream, fresh raspberries and a tart-tasting raspberry coulis and topped with a layer of chocolate fudge icing. Chocolate-cake purists can leave out the raspberries if preferred.

125g self-raising flour
25g cocoa powder
1 tsp baking powder
125g butter, softened, plus extra to grease
125g caster sugar
2 medium eggs
1 tsp vanilla essence

For the icing
150g Sainsbury's Taste The Difference Belgian Fairtrade dark chocolate
25g unsalted butter
2 tbsp milk
125g icing sugar

For the filling
200g raspberries
1 tbsp icing sugar
200ml Sainsbury's double cream

PER SERVING
466 cals
29.5g fat
17.5g saturated fat
36.8g total sugars
0.55g salt

PREHEAT THE OVEN TO 180°C/160°FAN/MARK 4. Grease and line the bases of two 19–20 cm sandwich tins.

SIFT THE FLOUR, COCOA AND BAKING POWDER into a bowl. Add the butter, sugar, eggs and vanilla essence. Beat, using an electric whisk, for 2 minutes until smooth and paler in colour. Divide the mixture between the prepared tins and level the surfaces. Bake for 20–25 minutes until risen and just firm to the touch. Turn out onto a wire rack to cool.

TO MAKE THE ICING, melt the chocolate in a bowl over a pan of simmering water, making sure the base doesn't touch the water. Once melted, stir in the butter and milk. Take the bowl off the heat and beat in the icing sugar to make a smooth fudge-like topping. Spread over the top of one of the cooled cakes.

FOR THE FILLING, put half the raspberries in a food processor and whizz to make a purée. Push through a sieve resting over a bowl and stir in half a tablespoon of icing sugar. Whip the cream with the remaining icing sugar in a bowl until just peaking.

PLACE THE UN-ICED CAKE HALF on a serving plate and spread the cream over the top. Scatter with the remaining raspberries. Drizzle over the raspberry puree, then top with the other half. Serve immediately.

223

CAKES, BISCUITS & BREAD

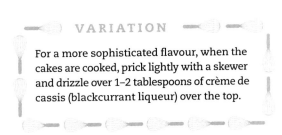

VARIATION

For a more sophisticated flavour, when the cakes are cooked, prick lightly with a skewer and drizzle over 1–2 tablespoons of crème de cassis (blackcurrant liqueur) over the top.

Ginger and Citrus Eccles Parcels

PREPARATION TIME: 35 MINS, *plus chilling* | **COOKING TIME: 12–15 MINS** | **MAKES 8** | ❄

Made from flaky, buttery pastry, these little parcels are filled with currants, citrus peel and a kick of spicy ginger. To enjoy them at their best, serve them freshly baked while they are still warm.

225g plain flour
pinch of salt
175g firm unsalted
   butter, cut into
   small dice
1 tsp lemon juice
beaten egg, to glaze
caster sugar, to dust

For the filling
175g Sainsbury's
   currants
25g Sainsbury's cut
   mixed peel
25g chopped glacé
   ginger
50g light muscovado
   sugar
finely grated zest
   of 2 lemons

PER SERVING
150 cals
7.8g fat
4.8g saturated fat
10.7g total sugars
trace salt

TO MAKE THE PASTRY, sift the flour and salt into a bowl. Add the butter, lemon juice and 100ml iced water. Using a round-bladed knife mix to a soft dough, adding a little extra water if it is too dry.

KNEAD LIGHTLY, then roll out on a lightly floured surface to a rectangle about 30cm long and 10cm wide. Fold the bottom third up and the lower third down, keeping the edges straight, then give the pastry a quarter turn. Repeat the rolling, folding and turning four more times. Wrap in greaseproof paper and leave to rest in the fridge for 30 minutes.

FOR THE FILLING, mix the currants, mixed peel, ginger, sugar and lemon zest together in a small bowl.

PREHEAT THE OVEN TO 220°C/200°FAN/MARK 7 and put two baking sheets in the oven to preheat. Roll out half of the pastry on a lightly floured surface to a 40 x 40cm square. Cut in half lengthways then cut in half horizontally to make four squares.

SPOON A PORTION OF THE FILLING into each pastry square (keeping back half the filling to use in the remaining pastry). Fold each corner of the pastry square into the centre to make a square parcel. Brush with the beaten egg and sprinkle with caster sugar. Repeat with the other half of the pastry and filling.

PLACE THE PARCELS ON A BAKING SHEET and bake in the oven on top of the preheated baking sheet – this ensures the bases will be crisp – for 12–15 minutes, until golden. Serve warm.

224

VARIATION

Replace the currants, peel and lemon zest with 125g chopped glacé cherries, 50g chopped blanched almonds and 25g grated marzipan to make cherry and almond cakes.

Cherry Streusel Slice

PREPARATION TIME: 20 MINS, *plus cooling* | **COOKING TIME: 40–45 MINS** | **MAKES 8 SLICES**

Mildly spiced and pleasantly sweet, this cake is reminiscent of a traditional fruit crumble. The generous filling of cherries in a syrupy vanilla sauce is encased in a buttery, almond crumble mixture and sprinkled with a similar topping. Serve sliced – with spoonfuls of natural yoghurt – as a teatime treat, or dessert if you prefer.

400g can stoned black
    or red cherries
2 tsp cornflour
1 tsp vanilla essence
175g self-raising flour
1 tsp ground cinnamon
grated zest of ½ lemon
125g unsalted butter,
    cut into small pieces
110g caster sugar
40g ground almonds
1 egg
icing sugar, to dust

PER SERVING
324 cals
16.9g fat
8.9g saturated fat
23g total sugars
0.2g salt

DRAIN THE CHERRIES, reserving 90ml of the juice. Mix a little of the juice with the cornflour in a small pan. Add the remaining juice and vanilla essence and place over a medium heat. Bring to the boil, stirring. Add the cherries and cook, stirring, for a further 1 minute until thickly coated in the syrup. Leave to cool.

PREHEAT THE OVEN TO 180°C/160°FAN/MARK 4. Line a 900g loaf tin with a paper loaf-tin liner.

PLACE THE FLOUR, cinnamon and lemon zest in a food processor. Add the butter and work until the mixture starts to cling together. Add the sugar and the ground almonds and process briefly until the mixture resembles a coarse crumble. (Alternatively, rub the butter into the flour, using your fingertips, then stir in the sugar and ground almonds.) Set aside about a third of the crumble mixture for the topping. Add the egg to the remaining mixture and mix to a fairly soft paste.

USE HALF THE PASTE to thickly line the base of the prepared loaf tin. Push the remainder up and around the sides of the paper to line it, pressing the mix down with a wooden spoon to fill any holes around the corners and in the base, to make a shell of dough mixture and line the base and sides of the paper.

SPOON THE CHERRY FILLING into the centre and sprinkle evenly with the reserved crumble. Bake for 40–45 minutes until the topping is pale golden.

LEAVE IN THE TIN TO COOL, then lift out using the paper edges. Put on a board and slice very carefully.

CAKES, BISCUITS & BREAD

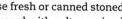 VARIATION

Use fresh or canned stoned plums, or apple slices layered with sultanas, in place of the cherries.

Hazelnut Meringue Gateau

PREPARATION TIME: 40 MINS, *plus cooling* **| COOKING TIME: 1½ HOURS | MAKES 10 SLICES**

Tiers of lightly spiced meringue – studded with white and dark chocolate pieces – form a delicious case for lightly whipped cream and a hazelnut praline. For a lighter gateau, replace half of the cream with thick Greek-style yoghurt or fromage frais. You can also increase the amount of spice if you prefer a more intense flavour.

125g shelled hazelnuts
5 Sainsbury's free range woodland egg whites
250g caster sugar
½ tsp ground mixed spice
75g Sainsbury's Taste The Difference Swiss white chocolate, chopped
75g Sainsbury's Taste The Difference Belgian Fairtrade dark chocolate, chopped
300ml double cream
cocoa powder, for dusting

For the praline
75g shelled hazelnuts
125g caster sugar

PER SERVING
510 cals
33.2g fat
13.6g saturated fat
47.4g total sugar
0.12g salt

LINE TWO BAKING SHEETS with non-stick baking parchment. Draw a 23cm circle onto one sheet, using a plate as a guide. On the other sheet, draw a 17.5cm circle. Turn the sheets over. Preheat the oven to 140°C/120°Fan/Mark 1.

TO MAKE THE MERINGUE, lightly toast the hazelnuts by placing them on a baking tray in the oven, then chop roughly. Whisk the egg whites in a bowl until stiff but not dry. Gradually whisk in the sugar, a tablespoon at a time, whisking well between each addition, until the meringue is stiff and very shiny. Whisk in the spice with the last of the sugar. Carefully fold in the chopped hazelnuts and white and plain chocolate.

SPOON THE MERINGUE ONTO THE CIRCLES, then spread neatly into rounds. Bake for about 1½ hours until dry and the undersides are firm when tapped. Turn the oven off and leave the meringues to cool in the oven.

FOR THE PRALINE, lightly oil a baking sheet. Put the hazelnuts in a small heavy-based pan with the sugar. Place over a gentle heat, stirring until the sugar melts. Continue cooking until the mixture caramelises to a rich golden-brown colour, then pour onto the baking sheet. Leave to cool and harden.

PLACE THE PRALINE IN A POLYTHENE BAG and beat with a rolling pin until coarsely crushed.

CAREFULLY TRANSFER THE LARGEST MERINGUE round to a serving plate. Whip the cream until softly peaking, then spread over the meringue. Scatter with the praline. Cover with the smaller meringue round and dust the top with cocoa powder.

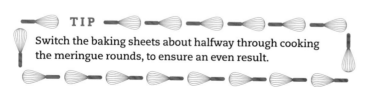

TIP
Switch the baking sheets about halfway through cooking the meringue rounds, to ensure an even result.

A Simple Loaf

PREPARATION TIME: 15 MINS, *plus rising and proving* | COOKING TIME: 30–40 MINS |
MAKES 1 LOAF (14 SLICES) | ❄

Everyone can have a go at making bread. For the best flavour it's important to leave the dough to rise and prove. When kneading, use oil on the work surface rather than flour so that you use exactly the right amount of flour for the loaf. Resist adding any more flour if the dough feels sticky – the rule for baking bread is the wetter the better, as this means the baked loaf will be lovely and light.

2 tsp dried active yeast
(see TIP, below)
500g Sainsbury's strong
white bread flour,
plus extra to dust
1 tsp salt
15g unsalted butter,
melted and cooled or
1 tbsp oil, plus extra
oil for kneading

PER SERVING
140 cals
2.4g fat
0.8g saturated fat
0.8g total sugars
0.35g salt

MEASURE 300ml lukewarm water into a jug and whisk in the yeast. Make sure it's completely dissolved in the water.

SIFT THE FLOUR INTO A BOWL and stir in the salt. Make a well in the centre and pour in the yeast mixture and the butter or oil. Mix together well to make a craggy dough – you may find it easier to use a table knife for this part. Tip out onto a clean work surface drizzled with a little oil and knead well for 10–15 minutes until soft and sticky. If the mixture feels dry, add another 50ml water.

PUT THE DOUGH IN A BOWL, cover with a pan lid big enough to fit on top of the bowl, or a clean tea towel, and leave to rise for about 45 minutes until doubled in size.

GREASE AND FLOUR A 900g loaf tin. Take the dough out of the bowl and gently knead again on a clean work surface with a little oil. Shape it into an oval then place into the prepared tin. Set aside to prove in a warm place for another 45 minutes. The dough can also be baked on a baking sheet. Shape into a round, slash with a knife and leave to prove as above. Preheat the oven to 200°C/180°Fan/Mark 6.

USE A BREAD KNIFE to slash diagonal lines across the width of the dough. Dust with a little flour then bake in the oven for 30–40 minutes until golden all over. To check the loaf is baked, tap the base: it should sound hollow. If it doesn't, return it to the oven for 5 minutes. Remove from the tin, cool on a wire rack and enjoy.

231

CAKES, BISCUITS & BREAD

VARIATION

For brown bread, use 350g wholemeal flour and 150g strong bread flour.

TIP

Dried active yeast is made by extracting all the moisture and looks like tiny beige balls. It needs activating in water before using. Fast-action yeast is also called easy bake and can be added straight to the flour. It doesn't need rehydrating in water first.

Fruit Bread

PREPARATION TIME: 20 MINS, *plus rising and proving* | COOKING TIME: 30–35 MINS |
MAKES 1 LOAF (16 SLICES) | ❄

This bread is ideal for breakfast, toasted and spread with butter, or for a teatime treat. It's made with a handful of dried fruit, a sprinkling of oats and mixed spice. To make into rolls, after the first rise, split the dough into 10 even-sized pieces (you can weigh them if it's easier) and shape into rounds. Put on a baking sheet, placed well apart, so they have space to expand when proving, then reduce the baking time to 15–20 minutes.

1½ tsp dried active yeast
500g strong bread flour
50g rolled oats
50g Sainsbury's Fairtrade golden caster sugar
75g Sainsbury's sultanas
25g Sainsbury's sour cherries, halved
1 tsp mixed spice
½ tsp salt
50g unsalted butter, melted and cooled

PER SERVING
142 cals
3.3g fat
1.7g saturated fat
7.8g total sugars
0.13g salt

MEASURE 350ml lukewarm water into a jug. Whisk in the yeast and make sure it has completely dissolved in the water.

SIFT THE FLOUR INTO A BOWL, then stir in the oats, sugar, dried fruit, mixed spice and salt. Make a well in the centre and pour in the yeast mixture and the butter. Mix together well to make a dough – you may find it easier to use a table knife for this part. Tip out onto an oiled board or clean worksurface and knead well for 10–15 minutes until soft and sticky. Put in a bowl, cover and leave to rise for about 45 minutes until doubled in size.

DUST A BOARD LIGHTLY WITH FLOUR. Take the dough out of the bowl and gently shape it into an oval. Grease a baking sheet with a little oil or butter then dust with flour. Put the loaf onto the baking sheet and leave to prove in a warm place for another 45 minutes. Preheat the oven to 200°C/180°Fan/Mark 6.

USE A BREAD KNIFE to slash diagonal lines across the width of the dough. Bake in the oven for 30–35 minutes until golden all over and the base sounds hollow when tapped.

TRANSFER TO A WIRE RACK TO COOL and enjoy in slices as it is or toasted with butter.

VARIATION

Use chopped mixed fruit or chopped dried apricots in the bread or simply vary the fruit mixture according to the ingredients you have to hand.

Sauces, Dressings & Dips

Basic White Sauce

PREPARATION TIME: 15 MINS | COOKING TIME: 10 MINS | SERVES 4

This classic sauce is made by stirring together melted butter and flour to make a paste (known as a 'roux') then stirring in milk to make a smooth sauce. It's the perfect base for a fish pie, either as it is or seasoned with freshly grated nutmeg and some chopped parsley.

25g butter
25g plain flour
300ml milk
salt and white pepper

PER SERVING
117 cals
8.1g fat
5g saturated fat
3.6g total sugar
0.2g salt

MELT THE BUTTER IN A SMALL PAN. Blend in the flour using a whisk and cook, stirring for 1 minute, to make a paste.

REMOVE FROM THE HEAT and gradually blend in the milk until completely smooth, whisking constantly.

RETURN TO THE HEAT and cook over a gentle heat, whisking constantly, until the sauce is thickened and smooth. Taste and season with salt and white pepper.

TIP

You can, of course, use black pepper rather than white to season the sauce, if that's what you have to hand, but the colour won't be as uniform white.

VARIATION

For a cheese sauce, stir in 50g grated mature Cheddar once the sauce has thickened. For a luxurious, creamy onion sauce, finely chop 1 small onion and cook with the butter over a low heat for about 15 minutes until softened. Stir in the flour and complete the recipe. Stir in 2 tablespoons of double cream and season well with salt and pepper.

SAUCES, DRESSINGS & DIPS

French Dressing

PREPARATION TIME: 5 MINS | SERVES 6

Adding a splash of water to an oil and vinegar base brings all the ingredients together more easily. This can be stored in the fridge for up to two weeks so you have a ready-made dressing to hand.

100ml vegetable oil
25ml white wine
    vinegar
2 tsp Dijon mustard
½ teaspoon sugar
½ shallot, finely
    chopped
salt and freshly ground
    black pepper

PER SERVING
115 cals
12.3g fat
1.7g saturated fat
0.7g total sugar
0.12g salt

PUT ALL THE INGREDIENTS APART FROM THE SHALLOT in a bowl and whisk well. Stir in the shallot and transfer to a clean, sealable jar. This will keep in the fridge for up to one month.

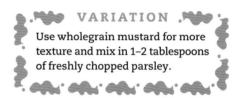

VARIATION

Use wholegrain mustard for more texture and mix in 1–2 tablespoons of freshly chopped parsley.

SAUCES, DRESSINGS & DIPS

Tzatziki

PREPARATION TIME: 10 MINS, *plus chilling* | SERVES 4–6

This fresh-flavoured dip is perfect with grilled chicken or lamb and couscous. It's important to squeeze out all the moisture from the cucumber otherwise the end result will be watery. Season generously with salt and pepper and taste again after chilling as this dulls the flavour.

½ cucumber, peeled, deseeded and grated
250g Greek-style yoghurt
½ garlic clove, crushed
2 tbsp extra virgin olive oil, plus extra to serve
1 tbsp freshly chopped dill, plus extra to serve
½ tsp salt

SQUEEZE ANY LIQUID OUT OF THE CUCUMBER and discard, then put the pulp into a bowl. Stir in the yoghurt, garlic, olive oil, dill and salt. Chill for at least 30 minutes to allow all the flavours to come together.

TASTE AND CHECK THE SEASONING before serving with a swirl of olive oil and a little extra chopped dill.

PER SERVING
46 cals
4.5g fat
1g saturated fat
0.8g total sugar
0.4g salt

VARIATION

With a couple of twists this recipe can easily be adapted to make raita, the traditional Indian accompaniment to hot dishes. Peel the cucumber and slice thinly and use plain natural yogurt and mint in place of the Greek-style yogurt and dill.

SAUCES, DRESSINGS & DIPS

Pesto

PREPARATION TIME: 5 MINS | SERVES 4–6 | ❄

This basil, pine nut and cheese sauce comes from the Liguria region of Italy and is perfect served simply stirred through hot pasta. For an economical and more waistline-friendly twist, use Grana Padano cheese instead. It's made with skimmed milk and costs less than Parmesan.

18g basil leaves
150ml olive oil
30g pine nuts, toasted
1 small garlic clove
50g Parmesan, grated
¼ tsp salt
freshly ground black pepper

PER SERVING
237 cals
24.3g fat
4.5g saturated fat
0.3g total sugar
0.3g salt

PUT ALL THE INGREDIENTS INTO A FOOD PROCESSOR and blitz until blended (you can use a pestle and mortar instead for this stage). Spoon into a sterilised jar and pour in enough oil to cover. The pesto can then be stored in the fridge for up to a week or frozen in a in a sealable container for up to 3 months.

TIP

The traditional Ligurian dish for pesto is pasta alla Genovese. To make this, place pasta in a large pan of boiling salted water, along with 1 large potato, cut into bite-sized cubes, and 200g trimmed, chopped green beans. Cook the pasta according to packet instructions, then drain and return the pasta and vegetables to the pan, with a couple of spoonfuls of the cooking water. Stir in the pesto and serve immediately with extra Parmesan and freshly ground black pepper.

243

SAUCES, DRESSINGS & DIPS

Hummus

PREPARATION TIME: 10 MINS | SERVES 4

This Middle Eastern dip makes the perfect relaxed starter served with toasted pitta and chunks of carrot, celery and pepper.

400g can chickpeas, drained well
juice of 1 lemon
1 tsp ground coriander, plus extra to serve
1 tsp ground cumin, plus extra to serve
2 tbsp tahini
2 tbsp olive oil, plus extra to serve
salt and freshly ground black pepper

PER SERVING
168 cals
11.7g fat
1.6g saturated fat
0.5g total sugar
0.35g salt

PUT THE CHICKPEAS, lemon juice, spices, tahini and olive oil in a food processor with 50ml cold water. Blitz to make a purée. Season with salt and pepper to taste then spoon into a bowl. Sprinkle over a little more ground coriander and cumin and drizzle with oil to serve.

TIP

To use dried chickpeas, soak them overnight in cold water, drain well and put in a pan. Cover with cold water, bring to the boil and simmer for 1–1½ hours until tender. Drain and complete the recipe.

EASY

Apple Sauce

PREPARATION TIME: 5 MINS | COOKING TIME: 5–10 MINS | SERVES 4–6 | ❄

This is a classic accompaniment to roast pork. Take care when adding the water – too much and the sauce will be watery; too little and the apple will dry out and stick to the base of the pan.

2 Bramley apples, peeled, cored and cut into chunks
1 tsp golden caster sugar
4 tbsp water
knob of butter
salt and freshly ground black pepper

PER SERVING
44 cals
1.5g fat
0.9g saturated fat
7.7g total sugar
trace salt

PUT THE APPLES IN A PAN WITH THE SUGAR and water. Cover with a lid and place over a gentle heat. Cook gently for 5–10 minutes until the apples break down and are pulpy. Check there is enough water in the pan halfway through cooking so the apple doesn't dry out and stir in 1 tablespoon of water at a time if it looks like it needs it. Add the butter, give the mixture a good stir and season well.

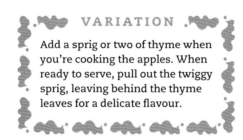

VARIATION

Add a sprig or two of thyme when you're cooking the apples. When ready to serve, pull out the twiggy sprig, leaving behind the thyme leaves for a delicate flavour.

247

SAUCES, DRESSINGS & DIPS

Mayonnaise

PREPARATION TIME: 10 MINS | SERVES 10

Although ready-made mayonnaise is easily available, making your own is a real treat and tastes very special. Take care when you're adding the oil at the beginning of the recipe; it needs to be added slowly, a drip at a time, until it emulsifies with the egg yolk. Once the mixture is thick, you can start to drizzle in the oil more quickly. Store in the fridge for up to two days.

2 medium egg yolks
½ tsp English mustard
100ml vegetable oil
100ml mild olive oil
squeeze of lemon juice
salt

PER SERVING
143 cals
15.7g fat
2.2g saturated fat
0g total sugar
trace salt

PUT THE EGG YOLKS AND MUSTARD IN A SMALL BOWL and whisk together using an electric hand whisk (you can also do this by hand with a balloon whisk, but it will take much longer and, of course, is quite hard work).

COMBINE THE OILS IN A JUG. Carefully add about 1 teaspoon of oil to the egg yolks. Whisk in quickly and continue to add the oil in this way, whisking between each addition, until the mixture thickens and looks creamy.

STIR IN A SQUEEZE OF LEMON JUICE and season with a little salt. Any mayonnaise that you don't eat straight away can be stored in the fridge for up to 2 days.

TIP

If the mixture splits, put another egg yolk in a clean bowl, whisk and slowly add to the split mixture, 1 tablespoon at a time, until the mixture emulsifies again.

VARIATION

For tartare sauce, stir in 3 chopped gherkins, 1 tablespoon of capers and 1 teaspoon of chopped tarragon. For aioli, the French version of garlic mayonnaise, stir in 1 garlic clove, which has been crushed to a purée.

249

SAUCES, DRESSINGS & DIPS

Custard

PREPARATION TIME: 5 MINS | COOKING TIME: 5 MINS | SERVES 4

The perfect accompaniment to a hot pudding. For a vanilla flavour, add 1–2 teaspoons vanilla extract or stir in the seeds from a vanilla pod.

1 medium egg yolk
1½ tbsp cornflour
2 tbsp golden caster
   sugar
300ml semi-skimmed
   or full-fat milk

PER SERVING
100 cals
2.6g fat
1.2g saturated fat
11g total sugar
0.11g salt

PUT THE EGG YOLK, cornflour, sugar and 2 tablespoons of the milk in a bowl and stir together with a wooden spoon.

POUR THE REMAINING MILK INTO A SMALL PAN and heat gently. As soon as bubbles appear around the edge, pour the milk onto the egg mixture. Stir everything together.

RINSE OUT THE MILK PAN, then pour the custard back into the pan and bring gently to the boil. Simmer for 2–3 minutes until the mixture thickens slightly and the mixture coats the back of the spoon. When you run your finger down the back of it and a line appears, it's ready.

VARIATION

To make a chocolate sauce, stir in 50g finely chopped good-quality milk chocolate after simmering the sauce.

TIP

If you're not going to use the leftover egg whites straightaway, you can freeze them in a sealable container for up to 6 months.

Hollandaise Sauce

PREPARATION TIME: 5 MINS | COOKING TIME: 15 MINS | SERVES 8

Poached salmon with a spoonful of buttery hollandaise sauce is a match made in heaven on a warm sunny day. Like mayonnaise, it's important to add the 'fat', in this case butter, slowly to the egg yolk at the beginning to allow the mixture to emulsify. Keep the heat really low underneath the pan so the mixture doesn't overheat and separate. If it looks as if it's going to separate, whip the bowl out of the pan and quickly whisk in 1 tablespoon of iced water. This will cool the mixture down immediately and bring it together again. If the hollandaise splits and can't be rescued, put a fresh egg yolk in a bowl and place over the pan. Beat well, then slowly add the curdled mixture, one spoonful at a time and it will magically come together.

1 small shallot,
    finely sliced
1 bay leaf
4 black peppercorns
50ml white wine
    vinegar
2 medium egg yolks
125g butter, cubed
    and chilled

PER SERVING
134 cals
14.2g fat
8.5g saturated fat
0.3g total sugar
0.24g salt

PUT THE SHALLOT, BAY LEAF and peppercorns in a pan with the white wine vinegar and bring to the boil. Simmer until reduced by half.

STRAIN THE LIQUID INTO A SMALL BOWL and add the egg yolk. Place over a small pan of barely simmering water, making sure the base doesn't touch the water. Whisk together, then start to add the butter, one cube at a time, whisking after each piece until the mixture thickens and becomes creamy.

VARIATION

For béarnaise sauce, add a sprig of tarragon and chervil to the white wine vinegar. Continue as above and after adding all the butter, stir in 1 teaspoon each of roughly chopped chervil and tarragon.

SAUCES, DRESSINGS & DIPS

Index

CONVERSION CHARTS

WEIGHT		VOLUME	
Metric	**Imperial**	**Metric**	**Imperial**
15 g	½ oz	25 ml	1 fl oz
25 g	1 oz	50 ml	2 fl oz
40 g	1½ oz	85 ml	3 fl oz
50 g	2 oz	150 ml	5 fl oz (¼ pint)
75 g	3 oz	300 ml	10 fl oz (½ pint)
100 g	4 oz	450 m	15 fl oz (¾ pint)
150 g	5 oz	600 ml	1 pint
175 g	6 oz	700 ml	1¼ pints
200 g	7 oz	900 ml	1½ pints
225 g	8 oz	1 litre	1¾ pints
250 g	9 oz	1.2 litres	2 pints
275 g	0 oz	1.25 litres	2¼ pints
350 g	12 oz	1.5 litres	2½ pints
375 g	13 oz	1.6 litres	2¾ pints
400 g	4 oz	1.75 litres	3 pints
425 g	15 oz	1.8 litres	3¼ pints
450 g	1 lb	2 litres	3½ pints
550 g	1¼ lb	2.1 litres	3¾ pints
675 g	1½ lb	2.25 litres	4 pints
900 g	2 lb	2.75 litres	5 pints
1.5 kg	3 lb	3.4 litres	6 pints
1.75 kg	4 lb	3.9 litres	7 pints
2.25 kg	5 lb	5 litres	8 pints (1 gal)